THE UNIVERSITY OF CHICAGO

INDIAN CITIES: CHARACTERISTICS AND CORRELATES

A dissertation submitted to the faculty of the Division of the Social Sciences in candidacy for the degree of Doctor of Philosophy

DEPARTMENT OF GEOGRAPHY

RESEARCH PAPER NO. 102

By

QAZI AHMAD

Department of Geography
University of Sind
Hyderabad, West Pakistan

CHICAGO · ILLINOIS

1965

PUBLISHED 1965 BY THE DEPARTMENT OF GEOGRAPHY, THE UNIVERSITY OF CHICAGO. PRINTED BY THE UNIVERSITY OF CHICAGO PRESS, CHICAGO, ILLINOIS 60637, U.S.A.

Library of Congress Catalog Card Number: 65-28148

TABLE OF CONTENTS

LIST OF TABLES

LIST OF TABLES.--Continued

LIST OF TABLES.--Continued

Table | | Page

LIST OF ILLUSTRATIONS

ACKNOWLEDGMENTS

I wish to express my gratitude to Professor Brian J. L. Berry whose seminars in quantitative methods and regional analysis furnished much of the background for the present study and under whose supervision and guidance it was undertaken and completed. Thanks are also due to Professor Norton S. Ginsburg and Professor Chauncy D. Harris for editorial and substantive suggestions.

I also wish to express my thanks to Miss Maureen Patterson and her staff for placing at my disposal all the necessary material that was available in the South Asian library.

I would like to thank my friends in the Geography Department, particularly Wallis Reed, Robert Murdie, Robert Tenant and Thomas Saarinen who helped me in many ways while this research was in progress.

Finally, deepfelt appreciation is extended to C. M. Naim, S. Shamimuddin Ahmad and S. Salman Nadvi for their many acts of kindness.

CHAPTER I

INTRODUCTION

General Objective

The pace of urbanization in India slowed down considerably during the census decade 1951-1961. The official census publication (Paper No. 1 of 1962) notes: ". . . one cannot help observing that even if none of the 1951 census towns were eliminated, the rate of urban growth during 1951-1961 would still have belied widely-held expectations of rapid increase."[1]

The percentage that urban population is of total population, used as a measure of degree of urbanization, during 1951-1961 remained almost stationary: 17.35 in 1951 and 17.95 in 1961.[2] This is true also of the total number of towns of all sizes which, however, was affected by changes in the definition of an urban area in the 1961 census.[3] Yet compared to 1951 there was a con-

---

[1]For examples of the population projections made before 1961 see Philip M. Hauser, "Implications of Population Trends for Regional and Urban Planning in Asia," United Nations Economic and Social Council, Working Paper No. 2 (E/CN.11/RP/L.21, July 2, 1958); Kingsley Davis, "Urbanization in India: Past and Future," in Roy Turner (ed.), _India's Urban Future_ (Berkeley: University of California Press, 1962), pp. 3-26; Samarendranath Mitra, "The Future of Population, Urbanization, and Working Force in India" (unpublished Ph.D. dissertation, Department of Sociology, University of Chicago, 1961), pp. 48-92.

[2]Urban population, here refers to the total population of towns of all sizes, as defined by the 1951 and 1961 Census of India. All statistical computations here and elsewhere relate to India excluding Jammu and Kashmir.

[3]According to the 1951 census, there were 3,057 towns in India, but as result of changes in the definition of an urban area in 1961, the number of census towns was reduced to 2,690. For more details, see Census of India, _Paper No. 1 of 1962, Final Population Totals, 1961 Census_, p. xxxv. This publication also outlines (p. xxxvii) the bases for determining a census town.

siderable absolute increase in both the number and population of medium and large size urban centers. Of particular interest are cities over 100,000 population. Their number increased from 73 in 1951 to 105 in 1961, an increase of about 44 per cent. No less important is the fact that 69 per cent of the decennial urban population increase occurred in cities of more than 100,000 population. These cities also accounted for about 45 per cent of the total urban population in 1961.

All this leads to the conclusion that while the pace of over-all urbanization in India has slackened during the past decade, the process of metropolitanization by the multiplication of large urban agglomerations has gained momentum. This phenomenon of metropolitanization has several implications, one of which is related to what has been described in urban literature as systems of cities. According to this concept cities are viewed as "systems--entities comprising interacting, interdependent parts."[1] It thus brings into focus such concepts as the rank-size rule and city size regularities and the related concept of urban hierarchy.[2]

It is evident from Figures 1 and 2 that, on the basis of 1961 census, the distribution of cities in India[3] conforms to the requirements of the rank-size rule. The linear relationship is

---

[1]See Brian J. L. Berry, "Cities as Systems within Systems of Cities," in John Friedmann and William Alonso (eds.), Regional Development and Planning (Cambridge: M.I.T. Press, 1964), p. 132.

[2]The rank-size rule refers to a statistical regularity which can be observed when, in any area, cities are ranked from the largest to the smallest according to population, and are then plotted on a graph. The size relationship in this case takes the form $P_r \cdot r^{-q} = K$, where q and K are constants, r is the rank of the city and P_r is the population of that city. The relationship is linear if the distribution is plotted on a logarithmic scale. See Brian J. L. Berry and William L. Garrison, "Alternate Explanations of Urban Rank-Size Relationships," Annals of the Association of American Geographers, XLVIII (March, 1958), 83-91, for a review of the basic literature.

[3]Cities over 100,000 in this case.

obtained no matter how "size" is interpreted.[1] This pattern has persisted for about half-century since 1921.[2]

The same concept is presented in another form in Figures 3 and 4. These contain best-fitting curves to city-size distributions in India in 1951 and 1961 respectively. In each the plot is of cumulative frequencies on lognormal probability paper. If city sizes are lognormally distributed, the resulting plot is a straight line.[3] The cumulative frequencies obtained were for cities with populations exceeding 20,000 and the cumulation proceeded over six size classes: 20,000-50,000; 50,000-100,000; 100,000-250,000; 250,000-500,000; 500,000-1,000,000; and over 1,000,000 to 100 per cent at the population of the largest city. Once again, using both definitions--political city and town group --we get a city-size distribution for India which tends to be lognormal. This is true of city-size distributions for both 1951 and 1961. In other words, in both years there is a linear relationship.

What are the implications of such a distribution of city-sizes? Berry, in his study of city size distributions and economic development, notes that:

> 1. A lognormal distribution is a condition of entropy, a circumstance in which the forces affecting the distribution are many and act randomly.

---

[1]The size of a city in Figure 1 refers to the population contained within the municipal limits of a city, while in Figure 2 size denotes the combined population of a _town group_ which in addition to a municipal city includes a cantonment area, if there is any, and residential and industrial suburbs and satellites. For more details, see Appendix A.

[2]Sovani has demonstrated that at least since 1921 Indian cities have conformed to the rank-size rule. N. V. Sovani, "Trend of Urbanization in India," in Indian Economic Association, _Papers Read at the 39th Annual Conference of the Indian Economic Association, 1958_ (Bombay, 1958), pp. 107-14.

[3]Brian J. L. Berry, "City Size Distributions and Economic Development," _Economic Development and Cultural Change_, IX (July, 1961), 575.

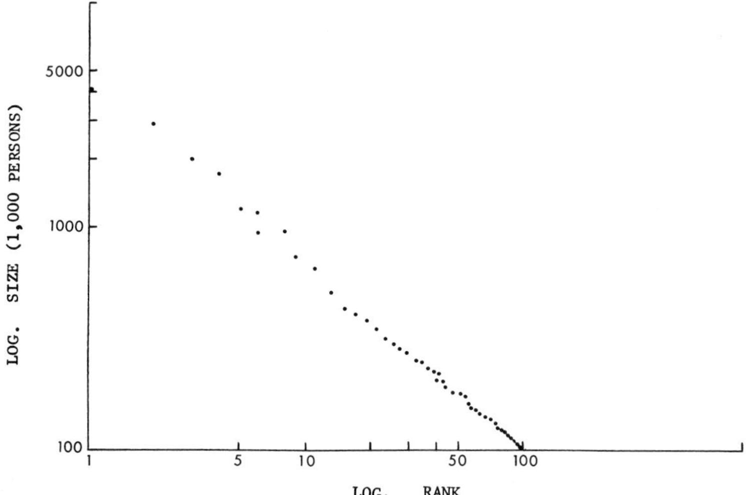

Fig. 1. -- Indian Cities (Political), Rank-Size Distribution, 1961

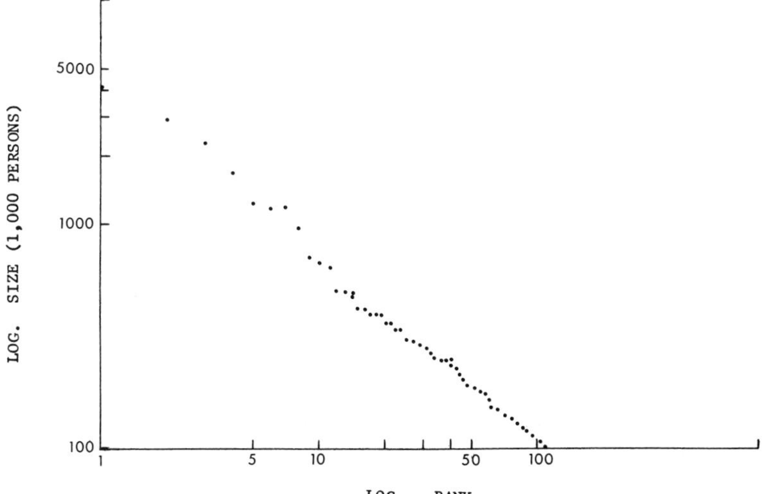

Fig. 2. -- Indian Town-Groups, Rank-Size Distribution, 1961

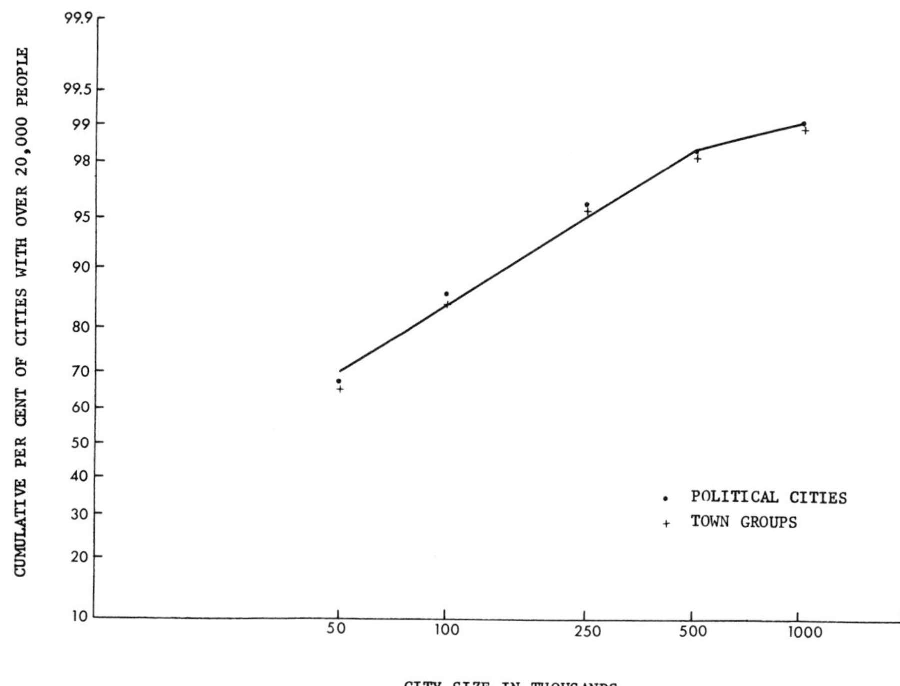

Fig. 3. -- City-Size Distribution in India, 1951

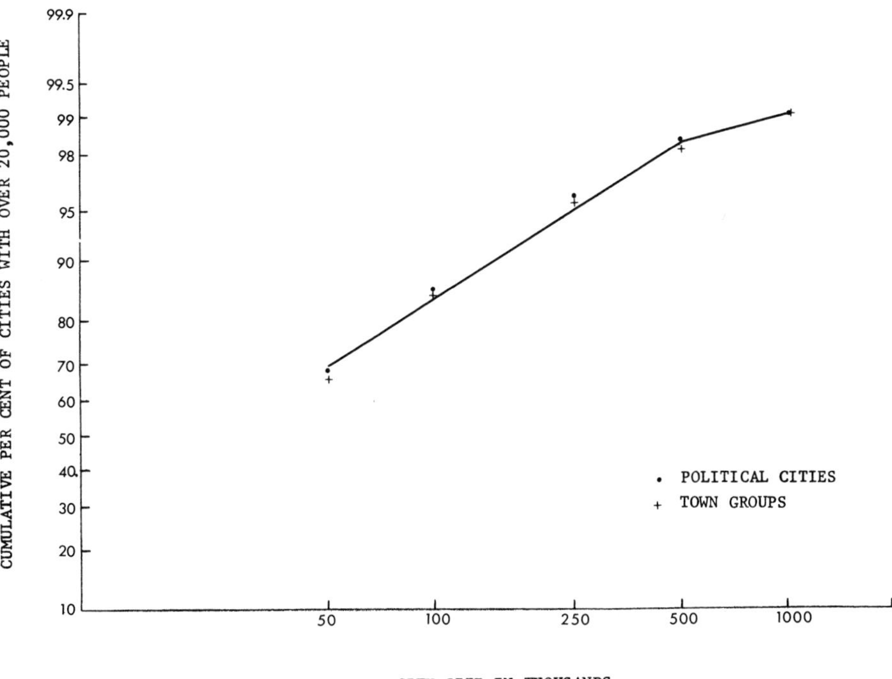

Fig. 4. -- City-Size Distribution in India, 1961

2. Rank-size distributions are found when, because of complexity of economic and political life and/or age of the system of cities, many forces affect the urban pattern in many ways, i.e., the above conditions of entropy obtain.

3. In the simple orderly cases most cities perform essentially the same set of functions--as complexity increases so do urban functions--political, as centers on transport routes, as specialized centers of primary or secondary economic activities, or as central places performing tertiary economic functions.[1]

Viewed in the light of these observations one can safely presume that Indian cities, which, as demonstrated above, tend to have a lognormal size-distribution and which conform to the requirements of rank-size regularity, are organized in a system comprising interacting, interdependent parts.[2] These cities perform a number of complex functions--political, as transport nodes, as specialized centers of industry, or as collecting and distributing centers. With increasing urbanization, there will be an increasing number of specialized cities performing one or the other or several of these functions, and this entire process ultimately could be responsible for the development of a metropolitan economy as witnessed in some of the highly urbanized and economically developed countries of today.

Inasmuch as these urban centers (Indian cities over 100,000) form a system and in that capacity affect the urban and economic structure of India, a research worker will be interested in properties of the members comprising the system. To determine critical properties is the aim of this study. Stated differently and in more explicit terms the objective is to discover dimensions of variation along which Indian cities can be arrayed. This is one way of acquiring an understanding of some of the major similarities

---

[1] *Ibid.*, pp. 582-83.

[2] See Britton Harris, "Urbanization Policy in India," *Papers and Proceedings, The Regional Science Association*, V (1959), 196.

and differences that characterize these relatively large urban agglomerations.

Generalizations Concerning the Nature and Function of Cities

Harris and Ullman summarized the classical principles of urbanism by recognizing three different types of cities.[1]

1. Cities as central places performing comprehensive services for a surrounding area.

2. Cities as transport foci and break-of-bulk points.

3. Specialized function cities performing one service such as mining, manufacturing, or recreation for large areas.

More recently Redfield and Singer introduced another classification of cities. Discussing the cultural role of cities, they recognized two types of cities:

> 1. Cities of orthogenetic transformation. These are of the moral order . . . of culture carried forward.
> 2. Cities of heterogenetic transformation. These are cities of the technical order, where local cultures are disintegrated and new integrations of mind and society are developed. . . .[2]

In addition, these authors recognized two patterns of urbanization: primary and secondary. In the primary phase a pre-civilized folk society is transformed by urbanization into a peasant society with correlated urban centers. This process takes place almost entirely within the framework of a core culture that develops in an indigeneous civilization. Secondary urbanization follows primary urbanization when a folk society, pre-civilized, peasant, or partly urbanized, is further urbanized by contact with

---

[1]Chauncy D. Harris and Edward L. Ullman, "The Nature of Cities," *Annals of the American Academy of Political and Social Science*, CCXLII (November, 1945), 7-17.

[2]Robert Redfield and Milton Singer, "The Cultural Role of Cities," *Economic Development and Cultural Change*, III (October, 1954), 53-73.

peoples of widely different cultures from that of its own members.

Hoselitz recognizes yet another set of cities on the basis of their role in the economic development of an area.[1] According to him a city is _generative_ if its continued existence and growth is one of the factors accountable for the economic development of the area in which it is located. It will be considered as _parasitic_ if it exerts an opposite impact. Further, in an attempt to tie together his ideas with those of Redfield and Singer he observes that although orthogenetic cities tend to limit, if not fully impede, cultural change, this does not mean that orthogenetic cities are necessarily parasitic with regard to economic growth.

Further, the process of primary urbanization, though leading to a reinforcement of existing cultural patterns, may be generative of economic growth. In the same way cities in certain stages of secondary urbanization may exert an unfavorable effect upon economic growth of the wider geographical unit of which they form a part. An example is that of colonial cities.

In a similar vein, Berry points out that the processes of secondary urbanization assert themselves when an integrated system of cities develops, usually under the influence of forces external to the local culture. "Heterogenetic cities result. . . . Complex nodal systems of economic organization characterized by rapid social change are the outcome."[2]

How relevant are these notions to an understanding of Indian cities? Do Indian cities fall into one of the four possible

---

[1]Bert F. Hoselitz, "Generative and Parasitic Cities," _Economic Development and Cultural Change_, III (April, 1955), 278-94.

[2]Brian J. L. Berry, "Urban Growth and Economic Development of Ashanti," in Forrest R. Pitts (ed.), _Urban Systems and Economic Development_ (Eugene: University of Oregon, 1962), pp. 53-54.

classes as mentioned by Hoselitz in his discussion of generative and parasitic cities?[1] In the opinion of this writer, and as most students of Indian urbanism would agree, Indian cities, like their counterparts in the Western world, are centers of heterogenetic transformations and are generative of economic growth. Also, the prevalent processes of urban growth in India display a pattern which is considered as secondary urbanization.

This, of course, is not intended to imply that there are no differences between the pattern of Indian urbanization, whatever it may be, and the urban patterns that exist in the Western world. During the past decade a number of studies have appeared which deal specifically with urbanization in the non-Western world.[2] The authors of these works suggest that urbanization in Asia may involve quite different patterns of development and interrelationships with economic development than those observed in the West. Some of the major differences indicated by them are: (1) urban development in many countries of Asia is largely an outgrowth of colonialism; (2) there is an increasing role of central planning and governmental interventionism in Asian economic development; (3) there are great differences in the ratio of population

---

[1]Hoselitz, op. cit., p. 280.

[2]Particularly interesting, as well as of great informative value, are the proceedings of the two seminars on urbanization in Asia and Latin America jointly sponsored by the United Nations and its agencies. See Philip M. Hauser (ed.), Urbanization in Asia and the Far East, ECAFE Region, Bangkok, 8-18 August, 1956 (Calcutta, 1957); Philip M. Hauser (ed.), Urbanization in Latin America, Proceedings of a Seminar Jointly Sponsored by the Bureau of Social Affairs of the United Nations, the Economic Commission for Latin America, and UNESCO, on Urbanization problems in Latin America, Santiago, Chile, 6-18 July, 1959 (New York, 1961). A recent essay by Norton Ginsburg focuses on the urban geographic literature as it pertains to Africa and, more particularly, Asia. See Norton Ginsburg, "Urban Geography and 'Non-Western' Areas," in Philip Hauser and Leo F. Schnore (eds.), The Study of Urbanization (New York: John Wiley and Sons, Inc., 1965). Also see Norton S. Ginsburg, "Urbanization in Asia," address delivered at Macalester College, St. Paul, Minnesota, March 20, 1959. (Mimeographed.)

to resources and the availability of open lands for surplus population emigration; (4) there are differences in basic outlook and value systems between Asia and the West.[1]

In addition to these differences, Britton Harris recognizes the fact that the developing nations are combining several stages of development in one era.

> They are using primitive, intermediate, and modern techniques together. Consequently, their range of specializations is greatly extended by comparison with the early stages of Western economic growth. In order to provide the economies of scale appropriate to the most modern sectors of the economy and culture, the size of cities in many non-Western countries is much larger than was the case in the early stages of European industrialization. Another factor contributing to the large size of cities in developing areas is the degree of urban unemployment, underemployment and employment in low-productivity service industries.[2]

These phenomena have contributed to the idea of "over-urbanization," which implies that the pace of urbanization is far more rapid than the normal rate of growth of economic development in the developing countries.[3]

Although Indian urbanization shares most of the characteristics common to other developing nations, it nevertheless has some distinctive features. To begin with, India has a long urban tradition which goes back more than a thousand years. In terms of absolute numbers, which no doubt is a function of size of total population, India has a huge quantum of urban population (78.8 million in 1961) which is distributed in some three thousand (2,690) urban centers of all sizes. Of these towns there were in 1961, 105 municipal cities including in some cases cantonment areas

---

[1]Hauser, _Urbanization in Asia and the Far East_, p. 31.

[2]Harris, _op. cit._, p. 196.

[3]See Kingsley Davis and Hilda Hertz Golden, "Urbanization and the Development of Pre-Industrial Areas," _Economic Development and Cultural Change_, III (October, 1954), 6-26; Hauser, _Urbanization in Asia and the Far East_, p. 9.

or 111 town groups.[1] Unlike many countries of the non-Western world, India has a well-developed urban hierarchy so far as city-size distribution is concerned. There is ample evidence to the effect that rural-urban migration is the most important factor contributing to urbanization in India.[2] As indicated by Bogue, this migration is directed not only toward the very large cities but also to hundreds of medium-size and smaller cities in almost all regions. Yet another point of significance is the fact, again mentioned by Bogue, that unemployment in the cities, rather than the restrictive effect of cultural tradition in the villages, is the major brake upon rural-to-urban migration at the present. With growing urbanization and rapid industrialization, there is a trend toward increasing specialization of function, with the result that there are now quite a few large centers of specialized activity, which did not exist a decade ago. A case in point is the emergence of new manufacturing towns of all sizes in the vicinity of major metropolises. Finally, Indian cities, like most Asian cities, are characterized by extreme congestion and overcrowding, a low female-to-male ratio, and a sizeable proportion of city population engaged in non-urban occupations.

Previous Approaches to Classification of Cities

Several attempts to study the occupational and employment structure of cities have resulted in well-known classifications largely on the basis of functional specialization, for example,

---

[1]According to the census definition, a city is one which has a population of 100,000 or over. For a discussion of town groups see Appendix A.

[2]See Kingsley Davis, *The Population of India and Pakistan* (Princeton: Princeton University Press, 1951), p. 114; Donald J. Bogue and K. C. Zachariah, "Urbanization and Migration in India," in Turner, p. 45; Hauser, *Urbanization in Asia and the Far East*, p. 136.

the studies of Harris, Pownall, and Duncan and Reiss.[1] In all of these schemes the aim of the authors is to seek an index or measure by which they can determine the intensity of specialization in a particular function of a city. In the earlier attempts to classify cities (e.g., Harris, Kneedler, Jones, Hart) a percentage is chosen at or above which a city is considered to be specialized in a particular function. Later attempts (Pownall and Nelson) display a search for more precise measures to determine the degree of specialization in a function. Pownall's use of simple deviations from the national average of a function or group of functions for cities of a particular size-class is based on the assumption that when a city in a particular size-class has an "abnormal" percentage of population in any single function (positive deviation from the national average), that city can be considered to be specialized in that function. Nelson's method is based on the same assumption as that of Pownall, although he (Nelson) employs the standard deviation as a measure of the intensity of specialization in a function.[2]

The only systematic work on functional attributes of Indian

---

[1]Chauncy D. Harris, "A Functional Classification of Cities in the United States," _Geographical Review_, XXXIII (January, 1943), 86-99; Grace M. Kneedler, "Functional Types of Cities," _Public Management_, XXVII (July, 1945), 197-203; John F. Hart, "Functions and Occupational Structures of Cities of the American South," _Annals of the Association of American Geographers_, XLV (September, 1955), 269-86; L. L. Pownall, "The Functions of New Zealand Towns," _ibid._, XLVII (December, 1953), 332-50; Otis D. Duncan and Albert J. Reiss, Jr., _Social Characteristics of Urban and Rural Communities, 1950_ (New York: John Wiley and Sons, 1965), pp. 12-16; Howard J. Nelson, "A Service Classification of American Cities," _Economic Geography_, XXXI (July, 1955), 189-210.

Prior to the first systematic classification of cities as presented by Harris, a number of attempts to determine the nature and function of cities had resulted in what may be described as non-statistical classifications such as those of Aurrousseau, McKenzie, Ogburn, and Hall--all familiar names in urban literature.

[2]Nelson's use of standard deviations in this case, however, is unfortunate, to the extent that the data to which this measure of variation is applied by him are not normally distributed.

cities is Lal's doctoral dissertation.[1] This study has an approach similar to that of Duncan and Reiss. Lal, however, follows a different method for classifying cities. He determines functional specialization of cities on the basis of "location quotients" (LQ's). He defines the LQ for city X in industry Y as:

$$\frac{\text{Per cent of all workers in city X in industry Y}}{\text{The median per cent of all workers in industry Y in all the cities}}$$

Then he decides to consider cities with LQ values between 90-109 in any industry or service as having a "normal" specialization in that function.

Both the earlier and the subsequent efforts at classification mentioned above suffer from lack of uniformity in the choice of measures of the degree of specialization of functions of a city. Their selection of the criteria of specialization, as the various authors themselves acknowledge, is largely arbitrary. The variation of criteria from one study to another is responsible for the variation in results, appropriately demonstrated by Duncan as follows:

> Thus in one study (Duncan and Reiss, 1956) Boston is described as a wholesale trade center with important educational and military functions; in a second (Alexandersson, 1956) the only "chief city-forming industry" given for Boston is non-durable goods manufacturing; in a third study (Nelson, 1955) Boston is identified as a center of finance, insurance, and real estate activity and no other; and in yet a fourth study (V. Jones, 1953) Boston is classified as a "diversified" city with retail trade predominant in comparison with manufacturing.[2]

---

[1]Amrit Lal, "Some Characteristics of Indian Cities of Over 100,000 Inhabitants in 1951, with Special Reference to Their Occupational Structure and Functional Specialization" (unpublished Ph.D. dissertation, Department of Geography, Indiana University, 1958). Also, see Amrit Lal, "Some Aspects of Functional Classification of Cities and a Proposed Scheme for Classifying Indian Cities," <u>National Geographical Journal of India</u>, V (March, 1959), 12-24.

[2]Otis Dudley Duncan, *et al.*, *Metropolis and Region* (Baltimore: John Hopkins Press; Published for Resources for the Future, 1960), p. 34.

Yet another limitation inherent in the methodology or methodologies of these functional classifications is that they are univariate. They were not designated to handle a huge mass of data pertaining to different aspects of city structure and life.

What, then, is the alternative? Before one is suggested, it is pertinent to define the tentative properties of a classification that we are looking for--a classification that makes sense. Briefly stated, such a classification should be multifactor or multivariable. Hence, it should probably be derived through use of multivariate statistical techniques. The use of generalized statistical methods will also enable research workers to achieve another objective, that of minimizing the area of human judgment and decision. An analytical procedure that guarantees use of standard measures also helps in comparing results obtained at two different points in time.[1] Furthermore, such techniques should "facilitate optimal allocation of newly observed individuals to existing groups,"[2] such that internal differences are minimized. This is essential if the object is to obtain relatively homogeneous groups. Finally, the optimality of classification and the relative homogeneity of groups should be verifiable through the use of standard statistical procedures such as discriminant functions, and the whole analytic procedure should result in identical results whoever applies them to the same set of data.

---

[1]See, for example, Sylvia Margaret Perle, "Factor Analysis of American Cities: A Comparative Study" (unpublished Master's dissertation, Department of Geography, University of Chicago, 1964). The purpose of this study was to compare the results of Price's analysis of American cities in 1930 with the 1960 distribution of cities in the same size class using the same fifteen criteria. Her findings were that the same underlying dimensions characterized American cities in both 1930 and 1960.

[2]Brian J. L. Berry, "A Note Concerning Methods of Classification," Annals of the Association of American Geographers, XLVIII (September, 1958), 300.

The first attempt to provide such a classification of cities was made by Moser and Scott.[1] Their object was to classify 157 British towns with populations greater than 50,000 in 1951, on the basis of 57 variables pertaining to population size and structure, population change, households and housing, economic characteristics, social class, voting behavior, health, and education. The procedure consists of preparing a 57 x 57 correlation matrix of the variables, followed by principal components analysis, which serves to extract the basic patterns according to which the towns vary. Finally, towns were grouped in several steps: (a) by visual means, adjacent points are grouped in the 2-space formed by the first two dimensions; (b) distances are measured from members of each group so defined to the group mean in 4-space; (c) towns were reallocated to groups at the margin, subject to the constraint of having at least ten towns to a group. This method of grouping does have certain weaknesses. The authors admit that their grouping of towns is arbitrary and that other methods might be more useful.[2] On the other hand, the British Towns study represents a major advance over earlier city classifications.

This study of Indian cities is directed toward developing a multifactor classification which incorporates all the properties of an optimal classification. An attempt is made to use appropriate multivariate statistical procedures where relevant, in addition to optimal methods of grouping, thus building upon the Moser and Scott methodology. Ray and Berry point out that the importance of these procedures is that they are analytic. "Decisions on the part of the investigator between preparation of a data matrix

---

[1]C. A. Moser and Wolf Scott, British Towns: A Statistical Study of Their Social and Economic Differences, Center for Urban Studies, Report No. 2 (Edinburgh: Oliver and Boyd, 1961).

[2]Ibid., pp. 88, 89, 93.

and formation of the groups are eliminated, for the entire process may be accomplished as a two or three phase run on an electronic computer. . . ."[1]

Organization

Chapter II begins with a discussion of the various multivariate statistical procedures used in this study. This is followed by a preliminary discussion of the sixty-two variables examined in the analysis--variables which cover a variety of the relevant aspects of urban structure in India. Finally, results of two factor analyses are given, with emphasis upon interpreting the underlying dimensions of variation in each case.

Each of the major dimensions of variation along which Indian cities vary was quantified, and, as a result, it was possible to develop an optimal classification comprising relatively homogeneous groups of cities. Results of the grouping analysis are presented in Chapter III, which also includes results of several discriminatory analyses.

The concluding section, Chapter IV, serves as a summary of the more pertinent findings of the study. It takes note of some of the major implications of these findings for understanding and further analysis of urbanization in India. In addition, results of similar studies recently completed in other Western and non-Western countries are compared with those produced for India.

---

[1]These procedures were utilized in a recent study of socioeconomic regionalization in Central Canada. See Michael Ray and Brian J. L. Berry, "Multivariate Socio-Economic Regionalization: A Pilot Study in Central Canada," paper presented at the Canadian Political Science Association Conference on Statistics, at Prince of Wales College, Charlottetown, Prince Edward Island, June 13-14, 1964, p. 4. Forthcoming in S. Ostry and T. Rymes (eds.), Regional Statistical Studies (Toronto: University of Toronto Press, 1965).

CHAPTER II

FACTOR STRUCTURE

Summary

What are the basic kinds of differences that exist among Indian cities? What dimensions shape India's urban system? Many variables relating to the population, housing, social, occupational, migration, spatial, and other characteristics of the cities may be studied and "boiled down" to answer this question. In what follows, sixty-two such variables are studied in their simultaneous co-variation, a far larger number than has ever before been assembled for Indian cities and studied together, and it is shown that there are ten general kinds of differentiations underlying these sixty-two and responsible for the correlations among them. The first several apply to all cities, whereas later kinds refer to smaller subsets of the whole, as follows:

I. The more southerly the location of the city the greater the female labor force participation in all occupations, the more balanced the sex ratio of the city, and the greater the proportion of in-migrants who come from rural areas.

II. The greater the accessibility to India as a whole of the area in which the city is located, the greater the size of the city (whether accessibility is measured as total population, industry, literate population, and the like), the more likely it is to be located in a cluster of cities of similar or larger size, the greater the total number of in-migrants (from other cities and rural areas), the greater the manufacturing employment, the greater the accessibility of the city to the railroad network, the lower the sex ratio (the cities are more male), the smaller the size of household, etc.

III. The greater the proportion of the labor force of the city in such tertiary activities as transport, service, and trade, the higher the proportion of telephone connections and banks per unit of population, the greater the distance of the city from metropolitan centers of over a million, and the smaller the proportion of workers in manufacturing and household industry.

IV. The greater the number of dwellings per unit area of the city and the higher the population density in the city, the smaller the area of the city, the higher the proportion of workers in trade and secondary industry, and the smaller the proportion of population in Scheduled Castes, or workers in primary activities such as mining, fishing and hunting.

V. The smaller the proportion of workers in primary industry, the greater the population of city, the more widely-spaced are the cities, the greater the manufacturing employment, the smaller the proportion of female in-migrants, and the lower the sex ratio of the city (manufacturing cities are more male).

VI. The smaller the population change between 1951 and 1961, the smaller the proportion of in-migrants in the age groups 0-14 years and 15-34 years, the smaller the proportion of workers in the city, the greater the proportion of in-migrants in the age groups 35-39 years and over 60 years, the greater proportion of female migrants, and the more balanced the sex ratio of the city.

VII. The more northerly the location of the city, the lower the literacy rate and the rate of population change between 1941 and 1951, the smaller the size of household and also the ratio of telephone connections and banks to the total population of the city.

VIII. The more easterly the location of the city, the smaller the proportion of in-migrants from other cities, the greater the proportion of in-migrants from rural areas, the greater the ratio of workers to the total population of the city, the smaller the proportion of female in-migrants, and the lower the sex ratio of the city (the cities are more male).

IX. The larger the city, the greater the proportion of in-migrants in the age groups 15-34 years, the smaller the proportion of in-migrants in the age group 0-14 years, the greater the distance from metropolitan centers of over a million, the higher the ratio of telephone connections to the population of the city, the higher the literacy rate, the larger the area of the city and the greater the accessibility of the city to the railroad network.

X. The higher the death rate and infant death rate, the higher the birth rate, the greater the proportion of population in Scheduled Castes, the larger the population of the city, and the smaller the size of household.

Outline of the Analytical Procedure

It is pertinent to outline the analytic procedure by which these generalizations, based upon fundamental dimensions of variation, are derived. Briefly, the steps are as follows: (1) Transformation of the scores of the n observations (cities) on each of the m variables (62 characteristics of the cities) such that all relationships are linear; (2) Principal components analysis of the m x m intercorrelation matrix of the m transformed variables and rotation of the resulting eigenvectors to a normal varimax position to satisfy the criterion of simple structure; (3) Computation of the factor scores of n observations on the r rotated factors; (4) Computation of pairwise indices of multifactor similarity of the cities. This involves measuring the distances between each pair of cities in the r-dimensional space created by locating the cities as points in a graph of the factors, and computing an n x n matrix of distances; (5) Stepwise grouping of the n observations using the distance measures, such that at every step maximum internal homogeneity of groups is ensured; (6) Iteration to check on the optimality of the grouping. This last phase is completed using discriminant functions.

The Model

The mathematical model employed to determine the underlying dimensions of variation is known as the principal components model.[1] The choice of components analysis is based on several considerations. The study of the covariance of economic, social, and demographic characteristics of cities is a problem of a multivariate nature. The multiplicity of variables found within large urban agglomerations makes for a vast complexity of relationships that required simplification in order to discover both the common and

---

[1]The method of components analysis owes its development to Harold Hotelling. See his article, "Analysis of a Complex Statistical Variables into Principal Components," The Journal of Educational Psychology, XXIV (September and October, 1933), 417-41, 498-520. For some of the more recent additions to literature on the component analysis, see the following items: H. H. Harman, Modern Factor Analysis (Chicago: University of Chicago Press, 1961), pp. 154-91; M. G. Kendall, A Course in Multivariate Analysis (London: Charles Griffin, 1957), pp. 10-36; Chester W. Harris, "Some Recent Developments in Factor Analysis," Educational and Psychological Measurement, XXIV (Summer, 1964), 93-206. For its application to problems of geographic and sociological nature, see Moser and Scott, op. cit.; a series of papers from Brian Berry who is perhaps the first geographer to have applied this technique including principal axes factor analysis, as well as direct factor analysis to problems of multifactor grouping and regionalization. See Brian J. L. Berry, "An Inductive Approach to the Regionalization of Economic Development," in Norton Ginsburg (ed.), Essays on Geography and Economic Development, Research Paper No 62 (Chicago: University of Chicago, Department of Geography, 1960), pp. 78-107; Ray and Berry, op. cit.; Brian J. L. Berry, "Identification of Declining Regions: An Empirical Study of the Dimensions of Rural Poverty," paper presented at the conference on Areas of economic stress, Queen's University, Kingston, Ontario, January 21 and 22, 1965 forthcoming in R. Thoman (ed.), Areas of Economic Stress in Canada (Toronto: Queen's University, 1965).

contrasting elements of the various groups of cities. This can be achieved if we utilize the technique of principal components analysis which treats the problem of the interdependence of many variables. In the study of interdependence, "we are concerned with the relationship of a set of variates among themselves, no one being selected as special in the sense of the dependent variate."[1] The essence of component analysis is to investigate how much of the total variability (in this case, between cities) exhibited in the primary variables can be accounted for by a smaller number of new independent variates, the so-called "principal components." These underlying factors or components can, at a later stage, be employed as the basis for a classification of cities.

The essential features of the components analysis are as follows.[2] After necessary transformations to ensure that such conditions as linearity and normality obtain, it will still be useful to eliminate the redundancies in the set of m variables by developing an orthogonal basis for the space in which the n observations are distributed. Each of the new orthogonal axes summarizes one pattern of intercorrelation of the m variables. Output from the component analysis includes a diagonal matrix of eigenvalues, Λ, two m x r matrices of "factor loadings" A, one for the principal axis solution, and the other for the analytic rotation of the principal axis solution to a "normal varimax" position and an n x r matrix of factor scores F, which provides a metric for locating the original n observations on each of the new r dimensions of the orthogonal basis.[3]

---

[1]Kendall, _op. cit_., p. 6.

[2]This section on the methodology of the components analysis draws extensively from the two last-mentioned studies in footnote 1 on the preceding page.

[3]"Orthogonal axes" implies a factorial solution in which

Thus, there are three initial matrices of interest:

X An n x m data matrix containing the scores of n observations on each of m variables.

Z An n x m matrix of the standard scores of each of n observations on m transformed variables.

R An m x m correlation matrix of each of the m transformed variables with every other.

The problem in a principal component analysis is to find a matrix A such that $R = AA^T$. This is accomplished by solving, using an iterative process, the eigenequation $(R - \lambda_1 I)\ a_1 = 0$ to produce a_1, the first column vector of A, then obtaining $(R - a_1 a_1^T)$ and solving for $[(R - a_1 a_1^T) - \lambda_2 I]\ a_2 = 0$. Repetition of the process r times yields the following output:

A An m x r matrix of "factor loadings" in which a_{kl} is the correlation of variable k with factor, or dimension l.

$a_1 a_1^T$ An m x m matrix showing that part of each of the intercorrelations of the m variables "reproduced" by the first factor or component.

AA^T An m x m matrix of "reproduced correlations" with 1 along the main diagonal.

---

the factors are uncorrelated (i.e., perpendicular); "factor loadings" are correlations of the original variables with the newly derived components; "eigenvalues" (Λ), which are the sum of squared factor loadings of the m variables with a component, tell the amount and proportion of variance of the original variables accounted for by each of the underlying dimensions; "communality," refers to the sum of independent common variances of the components on each variable, usually designated by the symbol h^2; "factor score" refers to the score or measurement of an observation on a factor or component. Joyce R. Royce in her paper, "The Development of Factor Analysis," The Journal of General Psychology, LVIII (July, 1958), 139-64, provides a useful glossary of terms used in factor analysis in Appendix A.

A variety of analytic solutions, orthogonal and oblique, for simple structure have been advanced in the last decade. Of these solutions, the "normal varimax solution" is probably the most widely used because it seems to give results which satisfy the requirements of the notion of "simple structure." See Henry F. Kaiser, "The Varimax Criterion for Analytic Rotation in Factor Analysis," Psychometrica, XXIII (September, 1958), 187-200; Henry F. Kaiser, "Computer Program for Varimax in Factor Analysis," Educational and Psychological Measurement, XIX (Autumn, 1959), 413-20.

$A^TA = \Lambda$ A diagonal matrix containing the l-th eigenvalue, λ_l in the l-th cell of the main diagonal. Each eigenvalue tells the amount of common variance of the m variables accounted for by each component. The fact that Λ is a diagonal matrix indicates that the cross-products of the r components are zero, i.e., that the components are independent.

In addition, the component analysis produces a matrix F of order m x r, such that $F = ZA\Lambda^{-1}$. Each f_{ij} is a factor score, the score given to observation i on factor j.

Rotation of the principal axis solution to a normal varimax position brings the solution close to Thurstone's concept of "simple structure," such that each of the original variables correlates highly with one and only one of the new dimensions. Thus, the principal components analysis yields a first component that accounts for the maximum variance, while the subsequent components account for decreasing proportions of the total variance.

Variables

The variables are measures calculated from the Indian census and from reports of other governmental and private agencies. Also included are the variables which are measures of clustering (such as distance to nearest city) and measures of relative accessibility such as different types of potentials. The latter were specially computed for the first time for this study. Operational definitions, sources of data, and the method of computation of these measures are provided in Appendix B.[1] The following list of sixty-two variables together with abbreviated names is provided to give an idea of their general nature at this stage:[2]

---

[1]The actual values of the variables for each town are provided in Appendix C, Table 51.

[2]Variables 54 to 62 were created by transgeneration; they are proportions of the absolute values, in each case, and not percentages.

1.	TOTPOPLATION	Total population
2.	AREAINSQMILS	City Area
3.	POPLNDENSITY	Population Density (Gross)
4.	POPCHGE51-61	Population Change, 1951-61 (Percentage)
5.	POPCHGE41-51	Population Change, 1941-51 (Percentage)
6.	SEXRATIO1961	Females per 1000 males, 1961
7.	SEXRATIO1951	Females per 1000 males, 1951
8.	LITCYRATE'61	Literates per 1000 population, 1961
9.	MALELITRAT61	Male literates per 1000 males
10.	DWELGPERSQML	Dwellings per square mile
11.	PERS100DWLGS	Persons per 100 dwellings
12.	PERS100HSHLD	Persons per 100 households
13.	BIRTHRATE'60	Birth rate, 1960
14.	DEATHRATE'60	Death rate, 1960
15.	INFNTDRATE60	Infant death rate, 1960
16.	MATNLDRATE60	Maternal death rate, 1960
17.	DISTCITYBYRD	Distance to nearest city over 100,000 by road
18.	DISTCTYBYRRD	Distance to nearest city over 100,000 by railroad
19.	DISTMCTYBYRD	Distance to nearest city over million by road
20.	DISTMCITYRRD	Distance to nearest city over million by railroad
21.	RAILRDROUTES	Railroad routes
22.	PRPSCHDCASTE	Scheduled Caste per 1000 population
23.	PCTOTWORKERS	Total workers as a percentage of population
24.	PCFEMWORKERS	Female workers as a percentage of total workers
25.	PCCULTVATORS	Percentage of cultivators

26.	PCAGRICLABOR	Percentage of agricultural laborers
27.	PCNTINMINING	Percentage of workers in mining, etc.
28.	PCINHOUSHOLD	Percentage of workers in household industry
29.	PCINMANUFCTG	Percentage of workers in manufacturing
30.	PCINCONSTRCT	Percentage of workers in construction
31.	PRCNTINTRADE	Percentage of workers in trade
32.	PCINTRANSPRT	Percentage of workers in transport
33.	PCINSERVICES	Percentage of workers in services
34.	PCFEMCULTVAT	Percentage of female cultivators
35.	PCFEMAGRLABR	Percentage of female agricultural laborers
36.	PCTFEMMINING	Percentage of females in mining, etc.
37.	PCFEMHOUSHLD	Percentage of females in household industry
38.	PCFEMMANFCTG	Percentage of females in manufacturing
39.	PCFEMCONSTRT	Percentage of females in construction
40.	PCNTFEMTRADE	Percentage of females in trade
41.	PCFEMTRNSPRT	Percentage of females in transport
42.	PCFEMSERVICE	Percentage of females in services
43.	PCPRIMINDTRY	Percentage of workers in primary industry
44.	PCSECINDSTRY	Percentage of workers in secondary industry
45.	PCTERTINDTRY	Percentage of workers in tertiary industry
46.	TELPER10000P	Telephone connections per 10,000 population
47.	BANKPER50000	Banks per 50,000 population
48.	POPPOTENTL61	Population potential, 1961

49. ROWCOORDNATS — Row coordinates

50. COLCOORDNATS — Column coordinates

51. URBANPOTENTL — Urban population potential

52. LITRATPOTNTL — Literate population potential

53. MFGPOTENTIAL — Manufacturing potential

54. PROPMIGRANTS — Proportion of migrants

55. PRPFEMMIGRNT — Proportion of female migrants

56. PRPMGAGE0-14 — Proportion of migrants aged 0-14 years

57. PRMGAGE15-34 — Proportion of migrants aged 15-34 years

58. PRMGAGE35-39 — Proportion of migrants aged 35-39 years

59. PRMG60+YEARS — Proportion of migrants aged 60 or over

60. PRPRURALMIGT — Proportion of migrants from rural areas

61. PRPURBANMIGT — Proportion of migrants from urban areas

62. PRUNCLASMIGT — Proportion of unclassified migrants

As would appear from the list of variables, an attempt has been made to compile as representative and wide-ranging a set of variables as was feasible.[1] These variables relate to the following attributes of Indian cities:

---

[1]Unlike many developing nations, India does have data-collection systems. However, most of the data are collected on the basis of administrative units such as states and districts. Consequently, statistical information on urban centers is either lacking or plainly deficient. Even an old and well-established organization like the Census of India, until 1951, had a very poor coverage of statistics on individual towns and cities. The trend seems to have changed recently, as the 1961 Census of India has a rather elaborate program of publishing a wide range of data, particularly on cities over 100,000 population. Thus, for the first time in census history, we will have information on housing and migration for all cities over 100,000 population. Also, much stress is being given to the collection and refinement of a more reliable set of vital statistics i.e., birth and death statistics.

1. Population size and structure (8 variables)
2. Population change (2 variables)
3. Households and housing (3 variables)
4. Occupational structure (23 variables)
5. Health (4 variables)
6. Spatial structure (11 variables)
7. Migration (9 variables)
8. Social amenities (2 variables)

So far as Indian cities are concerned, it is the first time that such a wide range of information has been brought together within the compass of a single study. Since one purpose of this study is to emphasize regional differences and spatial variations among Indian cities of different multivariate classes, a number of spatial variables derived from manipulation of the census data and from the direct measurement of distances on maps are included.[1] Also, for the first time, this study includes information pertaining to cityward migration.

Although the number of variables used in this study far exceeds that used in any of the previous studies of Indian cities, the coverage is by no means full and complete. To date, there is practically no information available on the age structure of city populations. Data pertaining to population change are inadequate. Housing statistics in the 1961 Census of India are meager. Occupational categories present a highly generalized picture of the occupational structure of cities. This list can be further extended, and many more loopholes can be spotted easily. However,

---

[1]Previous studies of city classifications, including that of Moser and Scott, have almost entirely ignored the spatial aspect of urban differentiation, a factor which is of foremost geographic interest. See Brian J. L. Berry, review of British Towns by C. A. Moser and Wolf Scott, in Economic Geography, XXXIX (April, 1963), 187-89.

with the availability of a wider range of more refined and reliable statistical information in the future, such a study as the present one can always be repeated, and the results, achieved at different points in time, can be compared.

The Components Analysis

The entire range of analysis as reported in this chapter, as well as in the subsequent chapters, was undertaken on the University of Chicago's IBM 7094-7040 computing system. The first phase of the analysis, which is concerned with the principal components analysis, was completed by using the program called MESA 84. As a first step, this program (MESA 84) edits the data and calculates univariate (means, standard deviations, skewness, etc.) and bivariate (correlations) statistics. The latter (correlation matrix), is then utilized by the factor sub-program of the MESA 84 system to obtain the principal components solution.

A preliminary run with untransformed data indicated high skewness in the case of a number of variables. In other words, a large number of the relationships involved were either non-linear or not homoscedastic.[1] In order to satisfy the assumptions of normality and linearity, the data were transformed into their logarithmic equivalents.

The transformed data were then reduced to a symmetric 62 x 62 correlation matrix (Table 48).[2] Since many of these 62 variables were interrelated, it was necessary to eliminate the redun-

---

[1]As Moser and Scott point out, the product-moment coefficient is a measure of linear association. If the condition of linearity is not satisfied, r will understate the actual degree of relationship. See Moser and Scott, op. cit., p. 59.

[2]Most of the correlations in this matrix are low, a phenomenon also noticed by Moser and Scott in their study of British Towns. According to them, the low correlations are a sign of the diversity of the British towns. The same can be said about Indian cities. See Appendix C.

dancies in the set of variables by developing an orthogonal basis for the space in which the 102 cities were distributed. The correlation matrix, therefore, was subjected to a principal axis solution which yielded 20 eigenvectors,[1] 10 of which were rotated to a normal varimax position.[2] These 10 components were also identified to have some recognizable significance.

The results of the component analysis are provided in Tables 3 to 13. Table 1 summarizes the proportion of the total intertown variance accounted for by each of the 10 components.

TABLE 1

INDIAN CITIES (POLITICAL)
PERCENTAGE OF TOTAL VARIANCE EXPLAINED BY EACH COMPONENT

Components	Eigenvalues	Per Cent of Total Variance
I	9.452	15.2
II	6.399	10.4
III	4.545	7.3
IV	4.135	6.7
V	3.917	6.3
VI	3.897	6.3
VII	3.471	5.6
VIII	3.413	5.5
IX	3.314	5.3
X	2.416	3.9
Per cent of communality over all the ten components		72.5

The ten rotated components together explain 72.5 per cent

---

[1]The program (MESA 84) extracts all of the eigenvalues of the input matrix and up to the 20 largest eigenvectors or components. For practical purposes this is quite a large number; in theory, however, it is always possible to extract as many factors as there are variables.

[2]Although the number of factors to be rotated may be specified by the user of the program (MESA 84) it is actually determined on the basis of specified minimums for the eigenvalues and/or the factor loadings. Accordingly, in this case, 10 out of 20 components were rotated because a cutoff criterion of $\lambda \geq 1 \cdot 0$ was pre-set.

of the total variance of the 62 variables. Thus, the variation between the towns, as contained in the 62 variables, can be attributed to 10 principal components, while the remaining components may be treated as minor terms of specific or random variance.

Table 2 shows the percentage of the variance of each primary variable accounted for by all 10 components. These values are the total sum of the squares of the correlations of a particular variable with all 10 components, in other words, communalities.

TABLE 2

PERCENTAGE OF VARIANCE (COMMUNALITY) OF EACH OF THE SIXTY-TWO VARIABLES ACCOUNTED FOR BY ALL TEN COMPONENTS

Variables (See previous list)	h^2 in Percentage	Variables	h^2 in Percentage
1	83.5	32	65.0
2	86.6	33	72.0
3	83.8	34	66.5
4	48.3	35	72.8
5	61.4	36	67.2
6	89.7	37	55.0
7	86.1	38	73.9
8	86.8	39	69.5
9	80.0	40	80.0
10	84.5	41	58.3
11	29.7	42	82.4
12	62.5	43	92.0
13	75.7	44	75.1
14	78.9	45	92.3
15	58.3	46	84.1
16	28.0	47	75.4
17	74.1	48	86.6
18	82.1	49	79.9
19	76.1	50	72.4
20	80.6	51	84.4
21	57.6	52	73.1
22	54.7	53	88.1
23	77.5	54	74.1
24	93.1	55	81.4
25	83.5	56	72.8
26	72.1	57	69.6
27	58.5	58	69.2
28	66.6	59	63.0
29	77.7	60	74.8
30	53.9	61	44.5
31	80.6	62	67.8

It is clear from Table 2 that some of the variables are better represented than others by the ten dimensions, so that the extent to which the components account for differences between the cities varies greatly between the variables. The variables least-well accounted for by the ten components are maternal death rates (28 per cent), persons per 100 dwellings (29.7 per cent), and population change, 1951-61 (48.3 per cent). On the other hand, the number of variables which are summarized quite well by the ten components is quite large. This implies that the variations of a large number of the sixty-two characteristics are effectively captured by the ten components, a desirable feature.

Components

Table 49 (Appendix C) provides a 62 x 10 matrix of factor loadings, which are correlations of each one of the sixty-two variables with the ten rotated components. The factor loadings give an idea of the strength of the relationship between a variable and a component.[1] In order to facilitate interpretation of the components, variables showing the highest correlations have been extracted for each of the ten components. What follows is a brief description of each of the ten components. The emphasis here is on the structure of the components, and on the strength and direction of the relationship between variables and the components. Their interpretation and implications in relation to the derived groups of towns will be discussed in Chapters III and IV, and of course, a simple overview of them constituted the introduction to this chapter.

The first component (Table 3), which accounts for 15.2

---

[1]Note that the signs have the same significance as in the correlation matrix. They indicate the direction in which the variable is related to the component.

TABLE 3

COMPONENT I: NORTH-SOUTH REGIONAL DIFFERENTIATION BY SEX

Primary Variables	Factor Loadings
Female workers as a percentage of total workers	0.843
Percentage of females in trade	0.843
Percentage of females in manufacturing	0.831
Percentage of females in services	0.807
Percentage of female agricultural laborers	0.758
Percentage of females in construction	0.744
Proportion of unclassified migrants	-0.719
Row coordinates	0.675
Proportion of migrants from rural areas	0.653
Percentage of females in household industry	0.650
Percentage of females in mining, etc.	0.627
Percentage of female cultivators	0.597
Percentage of females in transport	0.576
Females per 1,000 males, 1951	0.500
Females per 1,000 males, 1961	0.492

per cent of the total variance is identified predominantly with sex, and north-south regional differentiation. The highest factor loadings here belong to variables related to female labor force. Two other variables which show positive correlation with this component are the proportion of rural in-migrants, and the sex ratio of the city.[1] Inasmuch as the first component accounts for the

---

[1]The fact that there is a north-south differentiation of Indian cities based on their sex ratios was noted by Lal in his study of Indian cities. See Amrit Lal, "Age and Sex Structure of Cities of India," Geographical Review of India, XXIV (March, 1962), 7-29. Sen in his study of relatively small size towns (20,000-50,000 came out with the same finding. See J. C. Sen, "The Sex Composition of India's Towns with 20,000-50,000 Inhabitants, 1961," The Indian Geographical Journal, XXXVIII (July-September and October-December, 1963), 90-99.

largest proportion of the total variance, it should be considered as the most important single dimension of variation of Indian cities.

The high factor loadings associated with the second component are those related to different types of population potentials and to distance to the nearest city over 100,000 by road or railroad, both essentially measures of relative accessibility. The two are not obviously inter-correlated. Component II, therefore, should be identified mainly with accessibility within the country, a factor that produces conurbations. In addition, this component is also related to size of population, proportion of total in-migrants, size of household, sex ratio, banks per unit of population, manufacturing employment, railroad connectivity, and persons per dwelling. It is important to note the direction in which these variables are related to the component. (See Table 4.) Whereas total in-migrants, persons employed in manufacturing, and the number of railroad routes have direct relationship with the city size, other variables such as size of household, sex ratio, number of banks and persons per dwellings show negative correlations with the city size.

TABLE 4

COMPONENT II: CONURBATIONS AND ACCESSIBILITY

Primary Variables	Factor Loadings
Urban population potential	0.823
Population potential	0.791
Manufacturing potential	0.781
Distance to nearest city over 100,000 by railroad	-0.664
Literate potential	0.621

TABLE 4.--Continued

Primary Variables	Factor Loadings
Distance to nearest city over 100,000 by road	-0.574
Proportion of migrants	0.502
Percentage of workers in household industry	-0.498
Persons per 100 households	-0.492
Females per 1,000 males, 1951	-0.439
Total population	0.436
Banks per 50,000 population	-0.415
Percentage of workers in manufacturing	0.409
Railroad routes	0.408
Persons per 100 dwellings	-0.379

Component III, which represents the third most important dimension of variation, is associated with variables related to commercial and service structure of Indian cities. The most interesting aspect of this component is that it tends to differentiate centers of tertiary activity from centers of secondary industry. This is revealed by the signs of the respective factor loadings of the two groups of variables (Table 5). Also apparent is the fact that cities which specialize in service and commercial activity also have higher proportion of telephone connections and banks relative to population.

Component IV represents a dimension of compactness or the lack of it. It thus tends to differentiate two types of cities: those with relatively high population density and a high density of dwellings per unit area; this class of cities includes manufacturing and trade centers which often suffer from extreme congestion,[1]

[1]The city of Surat with 90,290 persons and 12,631 houses per square mile of area provides a good example.

TABLE 5

COMPONENT III: COMMERCIAL/INDUSTRIAL STRUCTURE

Primary Variables	Factor Loadings
Percentage of workers in tertiary industry	0.894
Percentage of workers in transport	0.723
Percentage of workers in services	0.635
Percentage of workers in trade	0.591
Telephone connections per 10,000 population	0.572
Percentage of workers in secondary industry	-0.564
Distance to nearest city over million by railroad	0.554
Distance to nearest city over million by road	0.529
Percentage of workers in manufacturing	-0.473
Banks per 50,000 population	0.456
Percentage of workers in construction	0.447

TABLE 6

COMPONENT IV: COMPACTNESS

Primary Variables	Factor Loadings
Dwellings per square mile	-0.833
Population density	-0.817
City area	0.681
Scheduled Castes per 1,000 population	0.567
Percentage of workers in secondary industry	-0.467
Percentage of workers in mining, etc.	0.466
Percentage of workers in trade	-0.439
Percentage of female cultivators	0.418
Percentage of workers in manufacturing	-0.414

as compared with the other class of cities with large areas and, therefore, low population and housing densities. Mining centers like Kolar Gold Fields and Dhanbad belong to the latter group. Also, the proportion of persons belonging to Scheduled Castes has a direct correlation with the area and a negative correlation with the population density of the city. (See Table 6.)

Component V isolates another pattern by which Indian cities are differentiated. It is essentially a rural component and as such emphasizes two groups of cities. These are: (a) those in which a relatively high percentage of population is engaged in non-urban functions such as agriculture and mining and (b) large cities and/or cities with considerable manufacturing. Cities in the first group show some clustering and have a more balanced sex ratio, a consequence of a higher proportion of female in-migrants. Though size of population loads only moderately on this component (0.4), there is some indication of a size differentiation (Table 7). Thus, most cities in the first group have relatively small size of population among 102 Indian cities of population greater than 100,000.

TABLE 7

COMPONENT V: RURAL ORIENTATION

Primary Variables	Factor Loadings
Percentage of workers in primary industry	-0.776
Percentage of agricultural laborers	-0.755
Percentage of cultivators	-0.742
Percentage of workers in mining, etc.	-0.412
Total population	0.402
Distance to nearest city over 100,000 by road	0.401
Percentage of workers in manufacturing	0.396
Proportion of female migrants	-0.389
Percentage of workers in secondary industry	0.345
Females per 1,000 males, 1961	-0.305
Females per 1,000 males, 1951	-0.303

The high coefficients associated with the sixth component are chiefly related to migration and per cent population change,

1951-61.[1] Further, the latter has a direct correlation with the proportion of total migrants. In other words, cityward migration was an important component of population change between 1951 and 1961. Thus, the component essentially summarizes population change during the period from 1951 to 1961. Note that the most active migrant age groups are 0-14 years and 15-34 years. The former, of course, imply the family type of migration, while the latter is related to single-member migration, and both are directly correlated with proportion of total migrants. On the other hand, the proportion of migrants in the age groups 35-39 years and 60+ years has an inverse relationship to the proportion of total migrants as revealed in this component (Table 8).

TABLE 8

COMPONENT VI: POPULATION CHANGE BETWEEN 1951 AND 1961

Primary Variables	Factor Loadings
Proportion of migrants aged 35-39 years	0.726
Percentage of population change, 1951-61	-0.651
Proportion of migrants aged 60 or over	0.626
Proportion of total migrants	-0.620
Proportion of migrants aged 0-14 years	-0.470
Total workers as a percentage of population	-0.441
Females per 1,000 males, 1961	0.434
Proportion of female migrants	0.431
Proportion of migrants aged 15-34 years	-0.420
Females per 1,000 males, 1951	0.315

Once again, the regional differentiation of Indian cities is underscored, this time, by Component VII.[2] The regional differ-

[1]As noted before, this is the first study of Indian cities which includes data on migration. However, the nature and quality of data are such that great care should be taken in interpreting results based on migration statistics.

[2]Note that "row coordinates" is one of the variables which are correlated with Component VII.

ence, in this case, is based on a number of social and economic factors such as literacy rate, telephone connections, and banks. However, except for the literacy rate, all other variables show low correlation coefficients with the component (Table 9). This implies that although there is no sharp boundary between the northern and southern cities, the two are differentiated, to a certain degree, on the basis of literacy rate, population change, 1941-51, and also such social amenities as telephone connections and banks.

TABLE 9

COMPONENT VII: NORTH-SOUTH REGIONAL DIFFERENTIATION OF LITERACY AND URBAN SERVICES

Primary Variables	Factor Loadings
Literates per 1,000 population	-0.847
Male literates per 1,000 males	-0.798
Percentage of population change, 1941-51	-0.532
Row coordinates	-0.425
Persons per 100 households	-0.417
Telephone connections per 10,000 population	-0.385
Banks per 50,000 population	-0.360

Another pattern of regional differentiation emerged on Component VIII, which shows that cities in the western part of India have a relatively high proportion of migrants from other urban centers, low proportion of migrants from rural areas,[1] low proportion of workers,[2] relatively high ratio of females to males in both 1951 and 1961, and higher proportion of female migrants (Table 10).

---

[1]Great care need be taken to interpret results based on migration statistics, particularly, those related to place of origin of in-migrants, since the percentage of unclassified in-migrants in many cases is quite high.

[2]On the other hand, most manufacturing centers including cities in the Calcutta conurbation with a high proportion of labor force are in the east.

Eastern cities had the converse. Again, it should be noted that there is no indication of a sharp division between the two regional groupings of cities.

TABLE 10

COMPONENT VIII: EAST-WEST REGIONAL DIFFERENTIATION OF MIGRATION CHARACTERISTICS

Primary Variables	Factor Loadings
Column coordinates	-0.697
Proportion of migrants from urban areas	0.642
Total workers as a percentage of population	-0.498
Females per 1,000 males, 1961	0.474
Proportion of migrants from rural areas	-0.441
Proportion of female migrants	0.433
Females per 1,000 males, 1951	0.413

The interpretation of Component IX, which explains a little over 5 per cent of the total variance, would be facilitated if it is read in conjunction with Component II, since the two in part, share a common theme (the size effect). While both the factors are related to size of population, they differ in their emphasis on distance relationships. Component II related conurbations whereas Component IX showed size of population to have a direct relationship to distance to the nearest city over a million.[1] A glance at the factor scores on this component confirms the belief that this component, in fact, reflects large city situations, with high proportions of migrants in the age group 15-34 years, large proportions of telephone connections, high literate poten-

[1]It may be pointed out that at least five of the seven million cities of India (i.e., Delhi, Calcutta, Bombay, Ahmedabad and Hyderabad) are at a considerably long distance from another city of similar size (i.e., over a million) by road or railroad. This factor alone must have affected the relationship between city size and distance to the nearest city over a million population.

tials, large area, and greater accessibility to the railroad network.[1]

TABLE 11

COMPONENT IX: SIZE OF POPULATION

Primary Variables	Factor Loadings
Proportion of migrants aged 15-34 years	0.675
Proportion of migrants aged 0-14 years	-0.668
Total population	0.592
Distance to nearest city over million by road	0.577
Telephone connections per 10,000 population	0.532
Distance to nearest city over million by railroad	0.523
Literate population potential	0.428
City area	0.417
Railroad routes	0.345

Components I to IX explain 68.6 per cent of the total variance of the sixty-two variables. The last of the ten recognized components explains only 3.9 per cent of the total variance. Because of the low factor loadings as well as the unreliable nature of Indian Vital Statistics,[2] interpretation of this component is not only difficult but hazarduous as well. Basically, this component is related to mortality and fertility rates. Other variables of some significance to this component are size of household, which has a negative correlation, proportion of Scheduled Castes, and size of population, both of which have positive but low correlations with birth and death rates. This pattern indicates that large size urban centers in India show relatively high rates of both fertility and mortality.

---

[1]Factor scores are discussed in Chapter III.

[2]However, the relationship as expressed here is not strong

TABLE 12

COMPONENT X: FERTILITY AND MORTALITY RATES

Primary Variables	Factor Loadings
Death rate, 1960	0.798
Infant death rate, 1960	0.690
Birth rate, 1960	0.589
Persons per 100 households	-0.339
Scheduled Castes per 1,000 population	0.323
Total population	0.217

General Evaluation of the Factor Structure

The principal components analysis of the sixty-two variables thus extracted ten major dimensions of variation of the 102 Indian cities.[1] (See Table 13.)

A general evaluation of the factor structure rests on a proper appreciation of the significance of the following points:

1. The factors or components have the important characteristic of being independent of each other, i.e., factors are not correlated with each other.

2. The factors are additive i.e., each component only tells part of the story, since it explains only part of the total variance. In the words of Moser and Scott, the components are "weighted averages of the primary variables, the latter contributing in very different degrees to the different components."[2] In the case of the first component, the weights are greater and therefore the association stronger, for those primary variables which are highly correlated with it. The other components, though ac-

---

enough to justify any generalization about the relationship of size of population and fertility and mortality rates in India.

[1]The names given to components reflect the general nature of the variables which show high correlations with the component.

[2]Moser and Scott, _op. cit._, p. 75.

TABLE 13

INDIAN CITIES (POLITICAL)
MAJOR DIMENSIONS OF VARIATION
(PERCENTAGE OF VARIANCE EXPLAINED BY EACH COMPONENT)

	Components	Per Cent of Variance
I.	North-south regional differentiation by sex	15.2
II.	Conurbations and accessibility	10.4
III.	Commercial/industrial structure	7.3
IV.	Compactness	6.7
V.	Rural orientation	6.3
VI.	Population change between 1951 and 1961	6.3
VII.	North-south regional differentiation of literacy and urban services	5.6
VIII.	East-west regional differentiation of migration characteristics	5.5
IX.	Size of population	5.3
X.	Fertility and mortality rates	3.9
Total percentage accounted for by Components I to X		72.5

counting for decreasing proportion of the total variance, add, bit by bit, to the complete or major part of the story. Furthermore, the fact that no less than nine factors account for a little over two-thirds of the total variance is understandable if we do not lose sight of the fact that this analysis was done on a very large and heterogeneous set of variables. An analysis based on a smaller and more homogeneous set of variables would probably result in fewer components.[1] However, the number of factors also reflects the great diversity of Indian cities at this stage of their development.[2]

3. Related to the above discussion is the significance of the input-output relationship in a component analysis. This implies that the "output" of a component analysis depends partly on the "input".[3] This point is also illustrated by the example mentioned above.[4] The input-output relationship has a bearing upon the generality of the results of a component analysis. How far the choice of variables has influenced the factor structure as obtained in this study is difficult to say. It seems, though, that most of the ten recognized components would probably emerge in any set of variables covering the major aspects of urban structure in India. However, components II, VII, and VIII would have disappeared in their present form had the variables relating to accessibility not been included in the analysis. This argument also

---

[1]In fact, a principal components analysis of 113 Indian town groups and twelve variables (total population, literacy rate, sex ratio, population change, 1951-61, one variable for each, and eight variables of occupational groups) yielded four components which together accounted for 99.9 per cent of the total variance; the first two accounted for 93.7 per cent.

[2]The fact that urbanization in India is passing through a transitional phase in the sense of historical development is quite important. At this stage, one finds in India all types of cities, the development of which is affected not by one or two or three factors but by many more factors--traditional, modern (western influence), colonial, regional and, above all, peculiar economic forces--all contributing to the present pattern of urbanization in India. So that we have cities as compactly built and crowded as Surat and Calcutta, cities with a significant proportion of population engaged in non-urban functions like agriculture, cities showing dominant regional characteristics, especially, in sex ratio, female participation in labor force, literacy, rate, and mode of migration, etc. More will be said about this situation in Chapter III.

[3]See Moser and Scott, _op. cit._, pp. 16, 76.

[4]See footnote 1 this page.

applies to the tenth component which is essentially related to fertility and mortality rates.

Consistency of the Components

Equally pertinent to this discussion is the consideration of the consistency of the components. This is very important, particularly insofar as the generality of the results is concerned.[1] The more crucial point in this connection is the consideration of the different ways to test the consistency of the components. It seems that this could be done in several ways, such as: (i) to repeat the analysis at another point in time, using comparable data; (ii) to divide India into subregions, e.g., Northern India and Southern India, and then carry out a separate component analysis for each section; (iii) to run several component analyses with variously defined units of observation e.g., the central city, and the metropolitan areas.[2] The last of these frameworks was applied in this study, to 102 town-groups as defined by the 1961 Census of India, with modifications in a few cases.[3] However, the analysis of town-groups is based on fifty-three variables instead of sixty-two used in the case of political cities. The difference is made up of the nine variables related to migration, for which data for

---

[1]More will be said about the consistency of the components in the last chapter.

[2]An example of the first type of testing procedure is Sylvia Perle's study of American cities, already mentioned. The second type of analysis is mentioned by Moser and Scott, who divided the 157 British towns into a "Northern" and "Southern" section, and then ran a separate component analysis for each section. Their finding was that the pattern of components was broadly similar for the two halves of the country. See Moser and Scott, *op. cit.*, p. 70. The third type of analysis is attempted here. These are the three possible ways, whose validity from the point of methodology might be questionable. It is hoped that research workers in geography, using the technique of factor analysis, will give due consideration to this aspect.

[3]See Appendix A.

several of the 102 town-groups were not available.[1]

In spite of the limitations of data and other differences in the two analyses as mentioned above, it is interesting to find that the factor structure as revealed by the component analysis of 102 town-groups is in no way markedly different from that obtained for the political cities (see Table 13). Ten rotated components together explain 74.2 per cent of the total variance of 102 town-groups on 53 variables. Table 14 lists the proportion of the total variance accounted for by each of the ten components.

No attempt is made here to discuss the factor structure of the town-groups in the details of the first analysis. Only major differences in the results of the two analyses will be outlined.

As already mentioned, the factor structure remains basically the same in both the analyses. However, Components III and IV in the town-group analysis account for higher proportions of the total variance than they did in the analysis of political cities. As a result, there is a shift in the relative dominance of the two components. Also, the third component--compactness--consists in the second analysis of variables which were divided between the fourth and fifth components in the first analysis. Another interesting change occurred in the structure of the second component which, in the town-group analysis, shows high correlations with the size of population and also with the "potential" variables. Similarly, the seventh component in the first analysis has moved up to occupy the fifth place in the second analysis.

---

[1]Also, the values of the fertility and mortality rates (four variables) for the town-groups are the same as those used for the political cities. Furthermore, errors in the computation of certain indices are simply unavoidable because of weaknesses inherent in the very definition of a town-group, as given in Appendix A. However, these are minor errors, and presumably have no major effect upon the results of the component analysis.

TABLE 14

INDIAN TOWN-GROUPS
MAJOR DIMENSIONS OF VARIATION
(PERCENTAGE OF VARIANCE EXPLAINED BY EACH COMPONENT)

Components	Per Cent of Total Variance
I. North-south regional differentiation by sex	15.3
II. Size of population	10.4
III. Compactness	9.0
IV. Commercial/industrial structure	7.5
V. Population change between 1941-51	6.7
VI. East-west regional differentiation based on degree of clustering around million city	6.0
VII. Dispersed cities (large inter-city distances)	5.3
VIII. Population change between 1951-61	4.8
IX. East-west regional differentiation based on proportion of banks and Scheduled Castes	4.6
X. Fertility and mortality rates	4.6
Total percentage of variance accounted for by Components I to X	74.2

These changes basically relate to the very definition of a town-group, which is obviously greater in size than the political city as it includes other municipal and non-municipal areas too. In some cases, like Calcutta, the population of the political city is 2.9 million while that of the town-group (greater Calcutta) is 6.1 million. No wonder, then, that both the factors of size and compactness have climbed up the ladder in the analysis of town-groups.

Finally, the factor structure of the town-groups is not quite as clear and easy to interpret as that of the political cities. This is particularly true of the last four components. This difference is probably due to a number of factors: the way town groups are defined; the crudeness of some of the data on town-groups; the way certain indexes have been computed; the fact that the units of observation in the second analysis consist of a mixture of town-groups and political cities.[1] Yet, the factor structure in both the analyses remains basically the same. This indicated that there is some consistency in the pattern of components which, as noticed before, are composite statements of the way Indian metropolitan centers differ from each other.

---

[1]Of the 102 observations, 46 are town-groups, and the remaining 56 are political cities.

CHAPTER III

CLASSIFICATION

Summary

Indian cities may be differentiated into several major groups on the basis of ten factors (and therefore on the basis of the original sixty-two variables). These statistical groups show a marked regionalization. The statistical analysis therefore has high geographic quality. The regional groups are:

(a) Northern cities, characterized by small female employment, low sex ratios, low literacy rates, relatively large proportions of persons belonging to Scheduled Castes, greater accessibility to the railroad network, small proportions of in-migrants, relatively small rates of population change, and low ratios of workers to population.

(b) Southern cities, characterized by greater female employment, more balanced sex ratios, larger proportions of female in-migrants from rural areas, higher literacy rates, lower accessibility to the railroad network, larger rates of population change, and higher proportions of in-migrants, as compared with Northern cities.

(c) Cities with generally central location (including most of the cities of Rajasthan, Madhya Pradesh, and a few cities of Maharashtra and other states of India, characterized by low generalized accessibility and a heavy concentration of tertiary activity.

(d) Calcutta suburbs, characterized by highly unbalanced

sex ratios, low female employment, heavy concentration of manufacturing activity, high ratios of workers to population, high potentials and relatively large proportions of in-migrants.

(e) In addition, there is a non-regional group of national metropolises, Bombay, Calcutta and Delhi (and perhaps also Madras and Hyderabad)--and of course, there are always the special cases, such as Gauhati and Kolar Gold Fields (as also Shillong and Durg town-groups).

The Grouping Procedure

The first step in the grouping procedure is to determine the degree of similarity of each pair of observations. This may be computed as distance between observations *i* and *j* in the space bounded by the dimensions of variation of the cities. Each city is located as a point in this ten-dimensional scatter diagram. A pair of observations which has identical scores on all dimensions lies at the same point; distance between the pair is zero. Close points are similar; distant points are dissimilar. Distances between points in the dimensions of the factor space, then, are multifactor indices of the similarity of the observations. If every pairwise distance is computed, it is possible to produce an n x n matrix D, an inter-observation similarity matrix, from the n x r matrix of factor scores F.

The next step is to apply a step grouping procedure to the matrix D, with a view to achieving a near-optimal classification of the observations into as many groups as are required, in the manner of the numerical taxonomist.

The distance matrix D contains n(n-1)/2 separate measures of similarity of the observations. Any grouping involves some loss of information about differences. The aim is to successively reduce the n one-member groups to n-1, n-2, . . . , 1 groups in such a way that at each step the loss of information is minimized. This objective is achieved in this way:

(1) Identify that pair of observations for which d_{ij}^2 is a minimum.

(2) Combine the row and column vectors of D represented by these observations into a single row and column vector representing the new group. The elements of these new vectors are the squared distances from the group centroid to all other points. The matrix D is now of order (n-1) by (n-1).

(3) Repeat the process to go from the n-1 groups to n-2, and so on, until a final pair of groups is linked into the entire population of observations. The result is a complete "linkage tree" which may be drawn to display the entire hierarchy of groups of observations. The tree proceeds from n outermost branches, through (n-1) and (n-2) to i and (i-1) to 4, 3, 2 and finally the main trunk 1. Associated with each level of grouping in the hierarchy is a measure of total within-group distance, and the loss involved in each successive step of grouping can be measured by the increment to this measure of loss (within-group variance or distance). The ratio of increment to total distance characteristically decreases in the grouping process to a minimum value, and then increases again. The step at which the minimum value occurs is usually a convenient point at which to pick groups for further study.

The final step involved in the grouping procedure is the use of iterative multiple discriminants which will force the near-optimal classification to converge to the optimal classification, such that within-group distance or variance is minimized and, by definition, between-group variance maximized.

Analysis of Factor Scores

Factor scores of the 102 Indian cities on the ten components allow these cities to be analyzed first with respect to the contribution of each component to their character. This gives a gross characterization, which may be followed by the grouping analysis itself. The cities with standard scores outside the range of ± 0.7 on each of the ten components are tabulated in Tables 18 to 27. A discussion of the factor scores in relation to various components will help in further elaborating the significance of the ten dimensions of variation as identified in Chapter II. The emphasis here (Chapter III) is on groups of cities reflecting high rankings on each one of the ten components. This discussion is intended to be as brief as possible. A more detailed discussion of the implications will ensue when the stepwise grouping of cities is completed.

The first component was identified predominantly with female occupational structure and the origin of in-migrants to the cities, both of which have a high positive correlation with the southern location. Accordingly, cities that rank high positive on this component are southern, whereas northern cities have high negative rankings. Further, the southern cities have relatively high percentages of females in the labor force, high female to male ratios and a high proportion of in-migrants from rural areas.

The second component was identified mainly with accessibility within the country, a factor that isolated conurbations and cities located within them. Cities that rank high positive on this component (Table 16) are large metropolitan centers with high

TABLE 15

CITIES WITH EXTREME FACTOR SCORES ON COMPONENT I

High Positive		High Negative	
Mangalore	2.14	Julludur	-2.20
Warangal	1.83	Saharanpur	-1.88
Malegaon	1.71	Amritsar	-1.85
Nagpur	1.63	Moradabad	-1.78
Eluru	1.62	Ludhiana	-1.75
Raipur	1.58	Patiala	-1.69
Salem	1.41	South Dum Dum	-1.69
Sholapur	1.38	Agra	-1.63
Guntur	1.30	Dehra Dun	-1.59
Tuticorin	1.28	Aligarh	-1.52
Kurnool	1.25	Bareilly	-1.51
Hyderabad	1.23	Asansol	-1.49
Alleppey	1.22	Shahjahanpur	-1.37
Vijayawada	1.14	Baranagar	-1.33
Rajahmundry	1.12	Rampur	-1.32
Jabalpur	0.99	Meerut	-1.27
Calcutta	0.97	Mathura	-1.22
Poona	0.95	South Suburb	-1.19
Madurai	0.94	Howrah	-1.04
Nasik	0.86	Garden Reach	-1.03
Nagercoil	0.85	Muzaffarpur	-0.96
Coimbatore	0.84	Kanpur	-0.87
Jamshedpur	0.72	Lucknow	-0.84
Udaipur	0.71	Kamarhati	-0.84
Tiruchirapalli	0.71	Cuttack	-0.82
Bombay	0.71	Bally	-0.79

degree of clustering. These cities also have large volumes of in-migrants, high proportions of workers in manufacturing, greater accessibility to the railroad network and characteristically, low female to male ratios.

Component III reflects a differentiation of cities based on their employment (secondary versus tertiary activity) structure. Accordingly, cities that rank high positive on this component are the cities which specialize in tertiary activity including political (administrative) functions. The majority of these cities are either state or district and division headquarters, port cities like Calcutta, Kakinada, Madras, Ernakulam, and Visakhapatnam, and railroad centers like Asansol and Ajmer (Table 17).

TABLE 16

CITIES WITH EXTREME FACTOR SCORES ON COMPONENT II

High Positive		High Negative	
Calcutta	3.89	Cuttack	-2.12
Bombay	3.09	Bikaner	-1.82
Howrah	2.00	Kurnool	-1.40
Bally	1.94	Surat	-1.38
South Dum Dum	1.70	Calicut	-1.35
Delhi	1.61	Mangalore	-1.35
Kamarhati	1.53	Jamnagar	-1.30
South Suburb	1.49	Darbhanga	-1.29
Thana	1.40	Jodhpur	-1.28
Baranagar	1.27	Belgaum	-1.25
Kanpur	1.15	Gorakhpur	-1.20
Vijayawada	1.08	Udaipur	-1.09
Nagpur	1.00	Ranchi	-1.09
Garden Reach	0.99	Muzaffarpur	-1.07
Madras	0.98	Sholapur	-0.91
Burdwan	0.98	Bhavnagar	-0.90
Bangalore	0.93	Bhagalpur	-0.85
Poona	0.92	Malegaon	-0.78
Nasik	0.90	Visakhapatnam	-0.76
Bhatpara	0.85	Trivandrum	-0.74
Raipur	0.83	Nellore	-0.73
		Ernakulam	-0.71

TABLE 17

CITIES WITH EXTREME FACTOR SCORES ON COMPONENT III

High Positive		High Negative	
Calcutta	2.72	Malegaon	-3.14
Burdwan	1.86	Bhatpara	-2.72
Kota	1.56	Garden Reach	-2.43
Bikaner	1.41	Sholapur	-1.93
Vijayawada	1.41	Bally	-1.92
Ajmer	1.29	Kamarhati	-1.79
Delhi	1.28	Jamshedpur	-1.78
Asansol	1.21	Surat	-1.64
Rajahmundry	1.18	Thana	-1.46
Jodhpur	1.13	Salem	-1.26
Raipur	1.13	Ahmedabad	-0.85
Kakinada	1.08	Bangalore	-0.80
Hyderabad	0.98	Baranagar	-0.76
Shahjahanpur	0.98		
Visakhapatnam	0.92		
Akola	0.86		
Allahabad	0.85		
Tuticorin	0.77		
Mathura	0.75		
Ernakulam	0.71		

On the other hand, cities than rank high negative on this component are those cities which specialize in secondary activity. Included in this category are the well-known manufacturing centers of India, such as Sholapur, Jamshedpur, Ahmedabad, Salem, and Surat. Most of these towns, as already noted in the preceding sections of this chapter, are close to one of the seven "million cities" of India.[1]

The fourth component represents a dimension of compactness or the lack of it. It thus tends to differentiate two types of cities. Cities with high negative rankings are the ones which show high population density and a high density of dwellings per unit area. This class of cities includes as many as thirty trade and manufacturing centers, with factor scores exceeding -0.7 (Table 18. As will appear from Table 51. these cities do suffer from extreme congestion, as compared with the other class of cities (with high positive rankings) which have relatively large areas, and therefore, low population and housing densities.

TABLE 18

CITIES WITH EXTREME FACTOR SCORES ON COMPONENT IV

High Positive		High Negative	
Kota	3.17	Moradabad	-1.77
Jodhpur	2.02	Belgaum	-1.70
Bangalore	1.82	Madurai	-1.57
Ranchi	1.64	Surat	-1.57
Ajmer	1.45	Rajahmundry	-1.41
Jamshedpur	1.41	Vijayawada	-1.37
Cuttack	1.41	Tiruchirapalli	-1.34
Kanpur	1.38	Ludhiana	-1.29
Jabalpur	1.36	Asansol	-1.22
Dehra Dun	1.28	Baranagar	-1.21
Udaipur	0.99	Salem	-1.21
Gwalior	0.98	Calcutta	-1.19
Warangal	0.98	Amritsar	-1.17

[1]There is a negative correlation between the two variables: per cent in manufacturing and distance to the nearest city over a million. See Table 8.

TABLE 18.--*Continued*

High Positive		High Negative	
Bhopal	0.94	Malegaon	-1.11
Delhi	0.93	Akola	-1.10
Nasik	0.73	Jamnagar	-1.10
Nagpur	0.71	Guntur	-1.07
		Eluru	-1.06
		Howrah	-1.04
		Vellore	-1.04
		Coimbatore	-1.02
		Shahjahanpur	-0.91
		Tuticorin	-0.86
		Baroda	-0.85
		Sholapur	-0.85
		Mathura	-0.80
		Hubli	-0.77
		Kamarhati	-0.75
		Nagercoil	-0.72
		Bareilly	-0.71

The fifth component was identified mainly with the non-urban occupational structure of Indian cities. It thus emphasizes two groups of cities. Cities that rank *high negative* on this component are the ones in which a relatively high percentage of population is engaged in non-urban functions such as agriculture, mining, fishing, etc. These cities also show a relatively large proportion of female in-migrants and a more balanced sex ratio. On the other hand, cities with *high positive* rankings have a larger population size, higher proportions of manufacturing employment, low proportions of workers engaged in primary activity and low sex ratios (are more male).

TABLE 19

CITIES WITH EXTREME FACTOR SCORES ON COMPONENT V

High Positive		High Negative	
Bikaner	2.30	Bandar	-1.95
Ahmedabad	2.04	Thanjavur	-1.62
Surat	2.02	Amravati	-1.62
Bhavnagar	1.83	Shahjahanpur	-1.62
Jodhpur	1.80	Raipur	-1.52
Jamshedpur	1.62	Akola	-1.46
Bhatpara	1.58	Nagercoil	-1.40

TABLE 19.--Continued

High Positive		High Negative	
Calcutta	1.55	Eluru	-1.37
Sholapur	1.54	Vijayawada	-1.24
Ajmer	1.36	Kolhapur	-1.22
Burdwan	1.34	Patiala	-1.21
Mangalore	1.31	Nellore	-1.20
Jaipur	1.31	Guntur	-1.14
Cuttack	1.19	Nasik	-1.13
Calicut	1.16	Darbhanga	-1.12
Hyderabad	1.12	Kakinada	-1.08
Madras	1.10	Patna	-0.96
Kamarhati	1.04	Belgaum	-0.94
Madurai	0.92	Meerut	-0.90
Kharagpur	0.85	Thana	-0.89
Garden Reach	0.82	Dehra Dun	-0.85
Howrah	0.78	Mathura	-0.82
Bombay	0.76	Muzaffarpur	-0.75
Baranagar	0.73	Kanpur	-0.74
		Kurncol	-0.70

Component VI is essentially related to population change during the period, 1951 to 1961, as a result of in-migration to cities. Accordingly, cities with high negative rankings on this component are the ones which show high rates of population change during 1951-61, large proportions of in-migrants and workers (in different occupations), and a low sex ratio. As against this, cities that rank high positive on this component are the ones which show relatively low rates of population change, small proportions of in-migrants, large proportions of female migrants, and a more balanced sex ratio (Table 20).

The seventh component reflects a regional differentiation of Indian cities based on literacy rates, population change during 1941-51, and such social amenities as telephone connections and banks. Thus, cities that rank high negative on this component are those cities which, with a few exceptions (Dehra Dun, South Suburb, South Dum Dum, Baranagar, Ranchi, Patiala, and Ludhiana), have a relatively southern location as compared to cities located in North India which, as shown in Table 21, have high positive rankings.

TABLE 20

CITIES WITH EXTREME FACTOR SCORES ON COMPONENT VI

High Positive		High Negative	
Calicut	2.78	Thana	-2.14
Alleppey	2.76	Bhopal	-2.12
Tuticorin	1.59	Bally	-2.07
Rampur	1.53	Malegaon	-1.57
Mirzapur	1.51	Vijayawada	-1.33
Trivandrum	1.40	Kurnool	-1.30
Shahjahanpur	1.32	Raipur	-1.26
Calcutta	1.31	Kamarhati	-1.03
Agra	1.05	Cuttack	-1.01
Madras	1.01	Ranchi	-1.00
Bhagalpur	1.00	Jabalpur	-0.96
Nagercoil	0.99	Jhansi	-0.96
Vellore	0.96	Visakhapatnam	-0.95
Varanasi	0.94	Belgaum	-0.94
Mangalore	0.93	Gorakhpur	-0.88
Saharanpur	0.90	Udaipur	-0.86
Moradabad	0.88	Patna	-0.84
Madurai	0.83	Guntur	-0.82
Gaya	0.81	Kota	-0.78
Aligarh	0.78		
Bhavnagar	0.78		
Indore	0.76		
Bandar	0.75		
Sholapur	0.72		
Mathura	0.71		
Ernakulam	0.71		

TABLE 21

CITIES WITH EXTREME FACTOR SCORES ON COMPONENT VII

High Positive		High Negative	
Shahjahanpur	2.32	Trivandrum	-2.65
Mirzapur	1.87	Ernakulam	-2.54
Rampur	1.77	Alleppey	-2.17
Bikaner	1.76	Calicut	-2.13
Bareilly	1.54	Dehra Dun	-2.07
Warangal	1.35	South Dum Dum	-2.00
Moradabad	1.34	Cuttack	-1.39
Jhansi	1.32	South Suburb	-1.37
Varanasi	1.29	Madras	-1.32
Kota	1.07	Thana	-1.25
Garden Reach	1.01	Baranagar	-1.21
Gaya	1.00	Coimbatore	-1.13
Kanpur	0.92	Tuticorin	-1.04
Kharagpur	0.89	Rajkot	-1.02
Malegaon	0.87	Bombay	-1.00
Eluru	0.87	Patiala	-0.98
Allahabad	0.86	Ranchi	-0.97
Bhatpara	0.84	Mangalore	-0.95
Raipur	0.84	Poona	-0.91

TABLE 21.--Continued

High Positive		High Negative	
Gwalior	0.80	Kolhapur	-0.89
Mathura	0.78	Nagercoil	-0.83
Sholapur	0.78	Ludhiana	-0.83
Lucknow	0.78	Ahmednagar	-0.82
Jabalpur	0.74	Baroda	-0.73
Bhagalpur	0.74		
Rajahmundry	0.73		
Darbhanga	0.71		

Cities in the first group (southern cities) compared with those in the north show higher literacy rates, higher rates of population change during 1941-51, larger household size and a higher ratio of telephone connections and banks to population.

Yet another pattern of regional differentiation emerges in Component VIII. This is clear from Table 22 in which cities with _high negative_ factor scores are those which have an eastern location, plus a relatively large proportion of in-migrants from rural areas, small proportions of in-migrants from other urban centers, large proportions of workers, small proportions of female migrants, and low sex ratios. The reverse holds for cities located in the western part of India.

The ninth component was identified predominantly with size. It reflects large city situation, with large proportion of migrants in the age group 15-34 years, large proportions of telephone connections, high literate potentials, large areas, and large numbers of railroad routes. This fact becomes more clear from Table 23 which provides a list of cities that rank high on this component. Note that cities which rank _high positive_ are mostly large-size urban centers. On the other hand, cities with _high negative_ rankings on this component are mostly small-size urban centers.[1]

[1]Note the words "large" and "small" are used here in relative terms. Hence, "large" means the larger of the 102 Indian cities over 100,000 population.

TABLE 22

CITIES WITH EXTREME FACTOR SCORES ON COMPONENT VIII

High Positive		High Negative	
Rajkot	1.71	Gauhati	-3.53
Agra	1.44	Calcutta	-2.77
Poona	1.40	Bhatpara	-2.39
Nasik	1.40	Garden Reach	-2.14
Thana	1.31	Bally	-1.96
Jaipur	1.23	Darbhanga	-1.85
Bangalore	1.20	Muzaffarpur	-1.65
Indore	1.19	Kolar Gold Fields	-1.45
Nagpur	1.16	Bhagalpur	-1.44
Bhopal	1.13	Gorakhpur	-1.37
Saharanpur	1.08	Howrah	-1.36
Jullundur	1.08	Tuticorin	-1.26
Ludhiana	1.08	Gaya	-1.25
Baroda	1.06	Patna	-1.13
Ujjain	1.04	Asansol	-1.03
Jhansi	1.02	Trivandrum	-0.97
Mysore	1.01	Nagercoil	-0.96
Moradabad	0.98	Cuttack	-0.87
Ajmer	0.98	Burdwan	-0.80
Delhi	0.91	Kakinada	-0.77
Bhavnagar	0.87	Calicut	-0.77
Hubli	0.86	Bandar	-0.75
Akola	0.85		
Coimbatore	0.83		
Jamnagar	0.82		
Bikaner	0.78		
Mathura	0.77		
Vellore	0.73		

TABLE 23

CITIES WITH EXTREME FACTOR SCORES ON COMPONENT IX

High Positive		High Negative	
Calcutta	2.72	Burdwan	-3.33
Delhi	2.61	South Suburb	-2.40
Bombay	2.38	Baranagar	-2.19
Patna	1.82	Kamarhati	-1.81
Ahmedabad	1.72	Kota	-1.73
Jabalpur	1.29	Eluru	-1.66
Gorakhpur	1.29	Tuticorin	-1.51
Lucknow	1.26	Rajahmundry	-1.48
Amritsar	1.14	Kharagpur	-1.35
Jullundur	1.07	Kakinada	-1.25
Ludhiana	1.06	Warangal	-1.18
Nagpur	1.02	Ajmer	-1.16
Gwalior	0.94	South Dum Dum	-1.11
Darbhanga	0.93	Bhavnagar	-1.09
Bangalore	0.85	Thanjavur	-1.07
Udaipur	0.82	Jodhpur	-1.06
Muzaffarpur	0.78	Vellore	-1.03

TABLE 23.--Continued

High Positive		High Negative	
Surat	0.77	Jhansi	-0.94
Hyderabad	0.76	Vijayawada	-0.89
Bhopal	0.75	Bhatpara	-0.86
Varanasi	0.74	Nasik	-0.74
Trivandrum	0.73	Cuttack	-0.73
Kanpur	0.70		

The tenth component is basically related to fertility and mortality rates. Other variables that are correlated with this component are household size which has a negative correlation, proportion of persons belonging to the Scheduled Castes, and population size, both of which have positive but low correlations with birth and death rates. This pattern indicates that large-size urban centers in India show relatively high rates of both fertility and mortality. This is corroborated from Table 24. Here cities that rank _high positive_ on the tenth component have larger population sizes as compared to those cities which rank _high negative_ on this component.

TABLE 24

CITIES WITH EXTREME FACTOR SCORES ON COMPONENT X

High Positive		High Negative	
Vellore	2.08	South Dum Dum	-2.55
Indore	2.03	Kharagpur	-2.52
Kanpur	2.00	Rampur	-2.49
Madras	1.99	Asansol	-2.03
Nellore	1.78	Jamnagar	-1.46
Coimbatore	1.51	Belgaum	-1.46
Varanasi	1.26	Bhagalpur	-1.46
Cuttack	1.25	Bikaner	-1.44
Madurai	1.22	Udaipur	-1.42
Salem	1.05	Mangalore	-1.42
Thanjavur	1.04	Warangal	-1.37
Visakhapatnam	1.03	Raipur	-1.36
Kurnool	1.03	Ernakulam	-1.31
Agra	0.99	Alleppey	-1.30
Bangalore	0.98	Gwalior	-1.04
Guntur	0.88	Bareilly	-0.98
Tuticorin	0.86	South Suburb	-0.97
Bhatpara	0.84	Bhopal	-0.87

TABLE 24.--Continued

High Positive		High Negative	
Surat	0.83	Hyderabad	-0.85
Ahmedabad	0.77	Hubli	-0.84
Rajahmundry	0.71	Thana	-0.82
		Patna	-0.79
		Kamarhati	-0.75
		Jamshedpur	-0.72

Results of the Grouping Analysis

The stepwise grouping of 102 Indian cities was computed by using the University of Chicago Social Science computer program called MESA 502. As a first step, this program produces an inter-city similarity matrix from the matrix of factor scores made available by the component analysis. The similarity matrix is then utilized by the "clustering sub routine" of the MESA 502 program to achieve a stepwise grouping of the observations (cities). The output of the grouping analysis contains a complete record of the way in which the grouping was accomplished and certain statistics computed at each stage which indicate both the degree of homogeneity of the groups and the amount of information lost in each simplification. More specifically, at each iteration the program computes three statistics--within-group variance, increment to within-group variance, and the ratio of increment to total within-group variance. This ratio characteristically decreases during grouping to a minimum value, and then increases again. The iteration at which the minimum value occurs is usually a convenient point at which to pick out groups for further study.

As shown in Table 25, the minimum value of R (ratio of increment to within-group variance) appears when the twenty-seven

[1]At each iteration of the grouping routine, the program prints out a list of the groups so far formed, lists of the members of each of these groups, and estimates of the information loss.

group solution is reached.[1] Beyond this point the value of R increases again. These twenty-seven-groups, therefore, represent the most homogeneous set of groups of 102 Indian cities (see Table 26-A'). At later stages in the grouping, more cities are included in fewer groups, but the groups are correspondingly less homogeneous and more diffuse. However, for all practical purposes, this is too large a number, particularly in view of the size of our sample (102 Indian cities). Hence, an eighteen-group solution seems to be an alternate choice, without doing much damage to the homogeneity of the groups (see Table 26-A).[2] The main consideration in the choice of eighteen-group solution as opposed to the twenty-seven is the relative ease with which eighteen groups can be handled.

TABLE 25

RATIO OF INCREMENT TO TOTAL WITHIN-GROUP VARIANCE

Number of Groups Formed	Increment to Total Within-Group Variance	Ratio of Increment to Total Within-Group Variance (R)
101	0.1248	1.0000
90	0.1626	.0906
80	0.1816	.0510
70	0.2002	.0365
60	0.2397	.0312
50	0.2802	.0271
40	0.3405	.0254
30	0.4037	.0236
27	0.4179	.0228
18	0.6041	.0261
10	0.9741	.0329
5	1.5389	.0428
3	1.8514	.0470
2	1.9732	.0477
1	2.0439	.0471

[1]These twenty-seven groups to which reference will be made later, include four single member groups, Calcutta, Kolar Gold Fields, Cuttack, and Gauhati (see Table 26).

[2]An attempt is made elsewhere in this chapter to underscore the main structural differences between these two group solutions, the twenty-seven-group solution and the eighteen-group solution.

TABLE 26

INDIAN CITIES (POLITICAL)
A MULTIFACTOR CLASSIFICATION INTO EIGHTEEN GROUPS

Eighteen Groups (A)	Twenty-seven Groups (A')
Group 1	
Bombay Delhi	Group 1
Calcutta	Group 24
Group 2	
Madras Indore Madurai Coimbatore Vellore	Group 2
Group 3	
Hyderabad Udaipur Nagpur Jabalpur Bhopal	Group 3
Jamshedpur Mangalore	Group 11
Warangal Kharagpur	Group 20
Group 4	
Bangalore Poona Nasik Thana	Group 4
Baroda Rajkot Mysore Ahmednagar Kolhapur	Group 14
Group 5	
Ahmedabad Sholapur Salem Surat Malegaon	Group 5
Group 6	
Kanpur Lucknow Allahabad Varanasi Mirzapur	Group 6
Group 7	
Howrah Bally Garden Reach Bhatpara	Group 7
Group 8	
Agra Saharanpur	

TABLE 26.--Continued

Eighteen Groups (A)	Twenty-seven Groups (A')
Aligarh Amritsar Bareilly Moradabad Mathura Shahjahanpur	Group 8
Gwalior Rampur	Group 13
Group 9	
Jaipur Jhansi Ajmer Jodhpur Bhavnagar Bikaner	Group 9
Kota Burdwan	Group 22
Group 10	
Patna Gorakhpur Muzaffarpur Ranchi Gaya Bhagalpur Darbhanga	Group 10
Group 11	
Ernakulam Trivandrum Calicut Alleppey	Group 12
Group 12	
Meerut Jullundur Ludhiana Dehra Dun Patiala	Group 15
Group 13	
Tiruchirapalli Ujjain Hubli Amravati Akola Raipur	Group 16
Vijayawada Guntur Rajahmundry Eluru Kakinada	Group 17
Tuticorin Thanjavur Nagercoil Bandar	Group 22

TABLE 26.--*Continued*

Eighteen Groups (A)	Twenty-seven Groups (A')
Group 14	
Visakhapatnam Nellore Kurnool	Group 18
Cuttack	Group 26
Group 15	
Asansol Jamnagar Belgaum	Group 19
Group 16	
South Suburb South Dum Dum Baranagar Kamarhati	Group 23
Group 17	
Kolar Gold Fields	Group 25
Group 18	
Gauhati	Group 27

Results of the Multiple Discriminant Analysis

The optimality of the groups derived through the stepwise grouping procedure was tested, using multiple discriminant analysis.[1] The results of the analysis are given in Table 27.

The discriminant analysis reclassified the marginally located observations in each group to achieve an optimal grouping of the r-space. The results of the analysis demonstrate clearly that the eighteen groups of 102 Indian cities derived through stepwise grouping procedure have attained near-optimality. The two changes that appear in Table 27 relate to two cities, Gwalior and Ujjain. The discriminant analysis has allocated Gwalior to Group 6, and Ujjain to Group 4. A reference to the factor scores of these cities will enable one to appreciate these changes. It would appear that Gwalior has definitely greater similarity to members of Group 6 as compared to those in Group 8. The same is true of Ujjain which, like other cities of Group 4, has high score on Component 8.

[1]A computer program written by Emilio Casetti was available at the computation center of the University of Chicago. For details see Emilio Casetti,"Multiple Discriminant Functions," Technical Report No. 11 of ONR Task No. 389-135, Contract NONR

TABLE 27

INDIAN CITIES (POLITICAL)
RESULTS OF THE MULTIPLE DISCRIMINANT ANALYSIS

Subsets with Cities	Iteration 1	Iteration 2
Subset 1		
Bombay	1	1
Delhi	1	1
Calcutta	1	1
Subset 2		
Madras	2	2
Indore	2	2
Madurai	2	2
Coimbatore	2	2
Vellore	2	2
Subset 3		
Hyderabad	3	3
Udaipur	3	3
Nagpur	3	3
Jabalpur	3	3
Bhopal	3	3
Jamshedpur	3	3
Mangalore	3	3
Warangal	3	3
Kharagpur	3	3
Subset 4		
Bangalore	4	4
Poona	4	4
Nasik	4	4
Thana	4	4
Baroda	4	4
Rajkot	4	4
Mysore	4	4
Ahmednagar	4	4
Kolhapur	4	4
Subset 5		
Ahmedabad	5	5
Sholapur	5	5
Salem	5	5
Surat	5	5
Malegaon	5	5
Subset 6		
Kanpur	6	6
Lucknow	6	6
Allahabad	6	6
Varanasi	6	6
Mirzapur	6	6

TABLE 27.--Continued

Subsets with Cities	Iteration 1	Interation 2
Subset 7		
Howrah	7	7
Bally	7	7
Garden Reach	7	7
Bhatpara	7	7
Subset 8		
Agra	8	8
Saharanpur	8	8
Aligarh	8	8
Amritsar	8	8
Bareilly	8	8
Moradabad	8	8
Mathura	8	8
Shahjahanpur	8	8
Gwalior	6	6
Rampur	8	8
Subset 9		
Jaipur	9	9
Jhansi	9	9
Ajmer	9	9
Jodhpur	9	9
Bhavnagar	9	9
Bikaner	9	9
Kota	9	9
Burdwan	9	9
Subset 10		
Patna	10	10
Gorakhpur	10	10
Muzaffarpur	10	10
Ranchi	10	10
Gaya	10	10
Bhagalpur	10	10
Darbhanga	10	10
Subset 11		
Ernakulam	11	11
Trivandrum	11	11
Calicut	11	11
Alleppey	11	11
Subset 12		
Meerut	12	12
Jullundur	12	12
Ludhiana	12	12
Dehra Dun	12	12
Patiala	12	12

TABLE 27.--Continued

Subsets with Cities	Iteration 1	Iteration 2
Subset 13		
Tiruchirapalli	13	13
Ujjain	4	4
Hubli	13	13
Amravati	13	13
Akola	13	13
Raipur	13	13
Vijayawada	13	13
Guntur	13	13
Rajahmundry	13	13
Eluru	13	13
Kakinada	13	13
Tuticorin	13	13
Thanjavur	13	13
Nagercoil	13	13
Bandar	13	13
Subset 14		
Visakhapatnam	14	14
Nellore	14	14
Kurnool	14	14
Cuttack	14	14
Subset 15		
Asansol	15	15
Jamnagar	15	15
Belgaum	15	15
Subset 16		
South Suburb	16	16
South Dum Dum	16	16
Baranagar	16	16
Kamarhati	16	16
Subset 17		
Kolar Gold Fields	17	17
Subset 18		
Gauhati	18	18

Interpretation of the Classification of Cities

The multivariate classification of Indian political cities resulting from the stepwise grouping of factor scores is given in Table 26. The distribution of the eighteen groups is shown in

---

1228 (26), Department of Geography, Northwestern University, Evanston, Illinois, 1946.

Fig. 6. While discussing each of the 18 groups of Indian cities, an attempt will be made to underscore the differences between the 18- and 27-group solutions, whenever necessary.

Group I consists of the three "National Metropolises"[1] of India--Bombay, Delhi and Calcutta--the only Indian cities with populations greater than two million. The common theme is the "size" effect. All three have high population potentials, high volumes of in-migrants, particularly those in the age-group 15-34 years, low sex ratios, greater accessibility to the railroad network, and the like. Although these cities have considerable industrial activity (especially in Bombay) they have, in fact, a more diversified economic base than many other cities with definite metropolitan functions.[2]

TABLE 28

GROUP I

Cities	Components									
	I	II	III	IV	V	VI	VII	VIII	IX	X
Bombay	71	309	- 22	47	76	- 31	-100	- 17	238	- 16
Delhi	- 52	161	128	93	68	- 60	- 46	91	261	38
Calcutta	98	389	272	-119	155	131	- 14	-277	272	- 17

In the 27-group solution (see Table 26), Calcutta stands out as a separate group. A glance at the factor scores (Table 28) helps identify some of the major differences between Calcutta on the one hand and Bombay and Delhi on the other. Unlike Bombay and Delhi, Calcutta has high scores on Components IV, V, VI and VIII. In other words, Calcutta has certain unique characteris-

[1]The term is borrowed from Duncan. See Duncan, Metropolis and Region, p. 90.

[2]Bombay and Calcutta have the largest concentration of port functions in India while Delhi plays a dominant role as a center of governmental activity. Note that the city of Delhi as defined here includes both Old and New Delhi.

KEY TO FIGURE 5

1. Amritsar
2. Jullundur
3. Ludhiana
4. Patiala
5. Saharanpur
6. Dehra Dun
7. Bikaner
8. Delhi
9. Meerut
10. Moradabad
11. Rampur
12. Bareilly
13. Aligarh
14. Shahjahanpur
15. Jodhpur
16. Ajmer
17. Jaipur
18. Mathura
19. Agra
20. Udaipur
21. Kota
22. Gwalior
23. Kanpur
24. Lucknow
25. Gorakhpur
26. Muzaffarpur
27. Darbhanga
28. Jhansi
29. Allahabad
30. Mirzapur
31. Varanasi
32. Patna
33. Bhagalpur
34. Gaya
35. Gauhati
36. Jamnagar
37. Rajkot
38. Ahmedabad
39. Ujjain
40. Bhopal
41. Jabalpur
42. Ranchi
43. Bally
44. Asansol
45. Burdwan
46. Jamshedpur
47. Kharagpur
48. Bhavnagar
49. Baroda
50. Indore
51. Surat
52. Malegaon
53. Akola
54. Amravati
55. Nagpur
56. Raipur
57. Cuttack
58. Nasik
59. Thana
60. Bombay
61. Poona
62. Ahmednagar
63. Sholapur
64. Hyderabad
65. Warangal
66. Visakhapatnam
67. Howrah
68. Rajahmundry
69. Kakinada
70. Elura
71. Vijayawada
72. Bandar
73. Guntur
74. Kolhapur
75. Belgaum
76. Hubli
77. Kurnool
78. Nellore
79. Mangalore
80. Bangalore
81 Kolar Gold Fields
82. Vellore
83. Madras
84. Mysore
85. Calicut
86. Salem
87. Coimbatore
88. Tiruchirapalli
89. Thanjavur
90. Ernakulam
91. Madurai
92. Alleppey
93. Trivandrum
94. Nagercoil
95. Tuticorin
96. Kamarhati
97. Baranagar
98. South Dum Dum
99. Calcutta
100. South Suburb
101. Garden Reach
102. Bhatpara

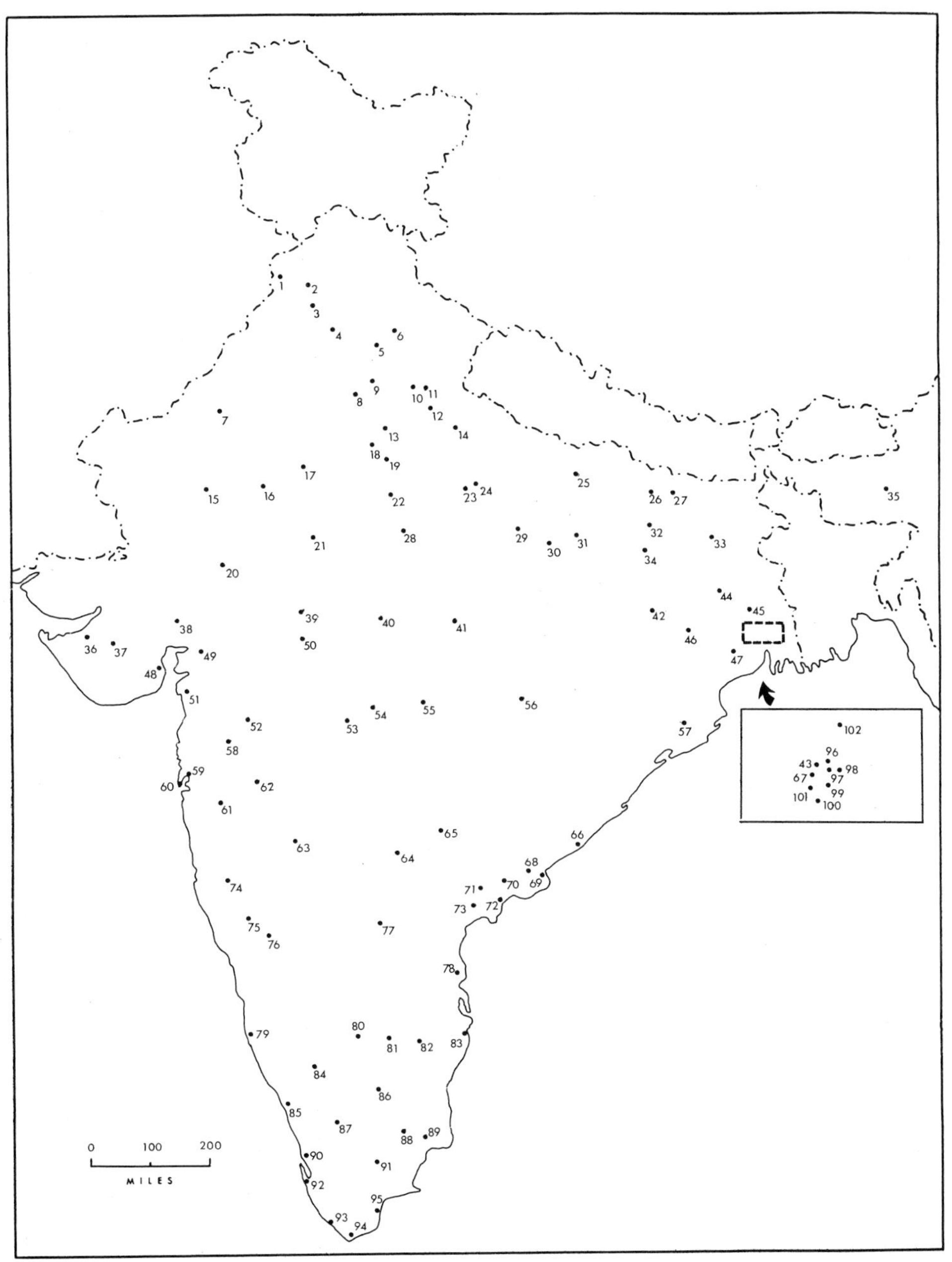

Fig. 5. -- Location of Indian Cities (Political), 1961

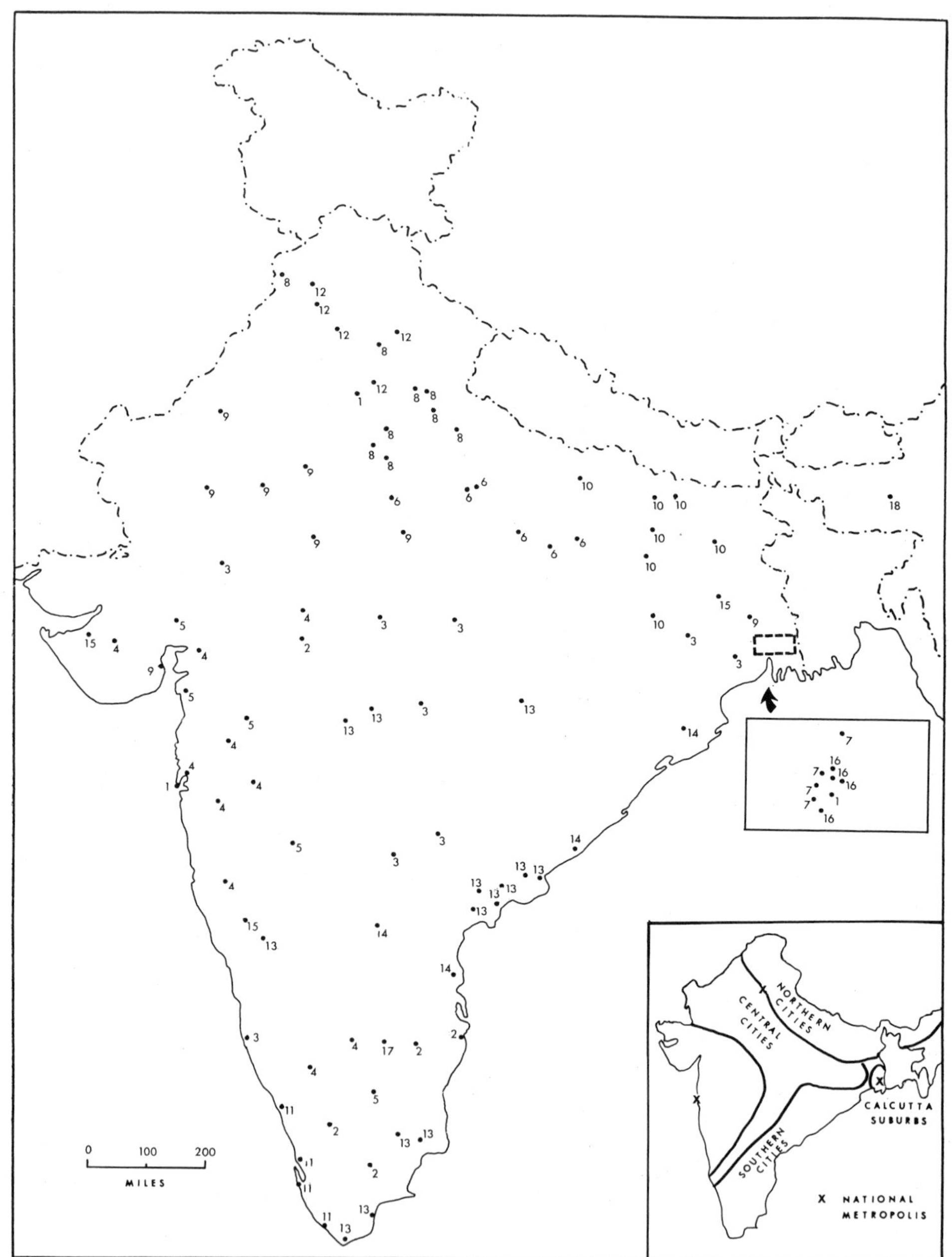

Fig. 6. -- Indian Cities (Political), A Multivariate Classification Based on 62 Variables

tics among India's major metropolises--extremely high densities of population and of dwellings per unit area, very low proportions of workers in primary activity (non-urban functions), extremely low rates of population change during the last two census decades, 1941-51 and 1951-61,[1] and very low sex ratios--much lower than those of Bombay and Delhi. However, the fact that at later stages of grouping Calcutta joins Group I shows that it has greater similarity to Bombay and Delhi than to other cities of India.

Group 2 contains Madras, Indore, Madurai, Coimbatore, and Vellore. The group as a whole has high scores on Components VII, VIII and X. However, it seems that the real basis of this particular grouping of cities is the tenth component (see Table 29). All the five cities have high mortality, infant mortality, and fertility rates. They are characterized by relatively small household size and large population (Vellore being the only exception). With the exception of Indore, all other cities have southern location, high literacy rate, large rates of population increase during the census decade 1941-51 and high ratios of telephone connections and banks to population, as revealed by Component VII. Furthermore, these cities are characterized by relatively high sex ratios, large proportions of female in-migrants, and large proportions of in-migrants from other towns.[2]

Group 3 contains altogether nine cities which, in general, have high scores on Components I and X (Table 30). These cities,

---

[1]Asok Mitra, the present Census Commissioner of India, has attempted an explanation of Calcutta's slow rate of growth during the past decade. See Asok Mitra, Calcutta, India's City (Calcutta: New Age Publishers Private Ltd., 1963), pp. 30-37.

[2]It is interesting to note that contrary to general impression, the city of Madras does not go with Group 1 but has affinities with cities which are much smaller in size. Unlike Bombay, Delhi, and Calcutta, Madras seems to display properties of a somewhat regional nature.

are characterized by relatively large proportions of women workers, large proportions of in-migrants from rural areas, and low mortality and fertility rates as indicated by negative scores on Component X.

TABLE 29

GROUP 2

Cities	Components									
	I	II	III	IV	V	VI	VII	VIII	IX	X
Madras	-21	98	58	42	110	101	-132	60	55	199
Indore	-29	38	-60	46	41	76	-57	119	45	203
Madurai	94	-24	8	-157	92	83	-46	23	16	122
Coimbatore	84	-21	-19	-102	24	-61	-113	83	40	151
Vellore	23	-59	-18	-104	16	96	-60	73	-103	208

TABLE 30

GROUP 3

Cities	Components									
	I	II	III	IV	V	VI	VII	VIII	IX	X
Hyderabad	123	15	98	45	112	34	52	34	76	-85
Udaipur	71	-109	53	99	60	-86	53	5	82	-142
Nagpur	163	100	12	71	35	-2	52	116	102	-18
Jabalpur	99	25	-4	136	-4	-96	74	48	129	-67
Bhopal	21	-7	55	94	-14	-212	65	113	75	-87
Jamshedpur	72	5	-178	141	162	-35	-25	-51	-7	-72
Mangalore	214	-135	-34	-49	131	93	-95	-36	35	-142
Warangal	183	24	-58	98	-51	23	135	-9	-118	-137
Kharagpur	17	59	42	1	85	-29	89	-34	-135	-252

According to the 27-group solution, Group 3 is made up of three separate groups: (1) Hyderabad, Udaipur, Nagpur, Jabalpur, and Bhopal, all of which have high scores on Components I, IV, IX and X; (2) Jamshedpur and Mangalore, both of which have high scores on Components I, III, V and X; (3) Warangal and Kharagpur with high scores on Components VII, IX, and X.

Group 4 contains nine cities, which, in general, have high scores on Components VII and VIII (Table 31). Ahmednagar and

Kolhapur are the only two exceptions, which unlike others in the group have low scores on Component VIII. Thus cities comprising this group are characterized by high literacy rates, large rates of population increase during 1941-51, relatively large household size, high ratios of banks to population, relatively southern and western locations, large proportions of in-migrants from other urban areas, relatively small proportions of workers, and a more balanced sex ratio. In addition, these cities, in general, have moderately high employment in manufacturing. This is particularly true of Thana, Baroda, and Bangalore, and to a lesser extent, Kolhapur, Poona, Rajkot, Nasik, and Ahmednagar.

TABLE 31

GROUP 4

Cities	Components									
	I	II	III	IV	V	VI	VII	VIII	IX	X
Bangalore	49	93	-80	182	-50	-54	-45	120	85	98
Poona	95	92	14	61	35	4	-91	140	8	-19
Nasik	86	90	-32	73	-113	-39	-69	140	-74	61
Thana	60	140	-146	55	-89	-214	-125	131	-13	-82
Baroda	-16	-47	-61	-85	59	-34	-73	106	41	23
Rajkot	-8	-44	-23	-13	-5	-43	-102	171	-22	-11
Mysore	1	-37	-17	40	5	59	-55	101	-49	-22
Ahmednagar	66	-40	-65	29	7	12	-82	8	-15	-26
Kolhapur	14	-32	-62	45	-122	23	-89	8	30	-33
Ujjain	29	61	-11	-7	-32	28	57	104	12	45

According to 27-group solution, Group 4 consists of two separate groups of cities: (1) Bangalore, Poona, Nasik, and Thana, all of which have high scores on Components I, II, IV, VII and VIII; and (2) Baroda, Rajkot, Mysore, Ahmednagar, and Kolhapur, with high scores on Components VII and VIII, and also on components II and III.[1]

[1]Note that while Bangalore, Poona, Nasik, and Thana have positive scores, the other group has negative scores, on Component II. The reason is obvious, since the former have very high

Group 5 consists of Ahmedabad, Sholapur, Salem, Surat, and Malegaon, the five most specialized manufacturing centers of India that have a relative western and southern location. All cities have high scores on Components I, III and IV, and a mixture of high and low scores on Component V (Table 32). This compact group of cities is characterized chiefly by a very high proportion of employment in manufacturing as well as in household industry, and relatively short distance to cities over a million population, in this case, Ahmedabad, Bombay, and Bangalore. In addition, these cities have relatively balanced sex ratios (except for Ahmedabad), very high proportions of rural in-migrants, high proportions of female employment (except in Ahmedabad), high population and housing densities,[1] and relatively small proportions of workers engaged in primary activity (non-urban functions).

TABLE 32

GROUP 5

Cities	Components									
	I	II	III	IV	V	VI	VII	VIII	IX	X
Ahmedabad	51	30	- 85	- 32	204	- 5	3	39	172	77
Sholapur	138	- 91	-193	- 85	154	72	78	42	40	15
Salem	141	- 69	-126	-121	35	9	63	17	21	105
Surat	63	-138	-164	-157	202	33	- 27	67	77	83
Malegaon	171	- 78	-314	-111	20	-157	87	46	25	- 27

Group 6 consists of Kanpur, Lucknow, Allahabad, Varanasi, Mirzapur and Gwalior.[2] These cities in general have high scores

---

potentials as in the case of Poona, Nasik, and Thana, and both high potentials and large size of population, as in the case of Bangalore.

[1]Surat with a population density of 90,290 is certainly the most congested city in India.

[2]Note that four of the five KAVAL (composite of the first letter of Kanpur, Agra, Varanasi, Allahabad, and Lucknow) cities are included in this group. These are major urban centers of

on Components IV, VII, X and I (Table 33).[1] On the whole, these cities are characterized by northern location, low literacy rates, low rates of population increase during 1951-61 and more so during 1941-51, relatively small household sizes, low proportions of female employment and low sex ratios, low densities of population and dwellings per unit area, relatively large proportions of persons belonging to Scheduled Castes, large area, relatively high mortality and fertility rates,[2] and greater accessibility to the railroad network, as most of them are important railway junctions.

TABLE 33

GROUP 6

Cities	Components									
	I	II	III	IV	V	VI	VII	VIII	IX	X
Kanpur	-87	115	-28	138	-0	-3	92	-14	70	200
Lucknow	-84	67	68	26	3	13	78	33	126	38
Allahabad	-30	27	85	60	21	53	86	-52	46	17
Varanasi	-28	1	2	42	32	94	129	-10	74	126
Mirzapur	27	-3	47	65	-42	151	187	-53	-21	47
Gwalior	-45	17	-53	98	-24	59	80	69	94	-104

Group 7 consists of Howrah, Bally, Garden Reach, and Bhatpara--four of the eight cities of the Calcutta conurbation.[3] The

---

Uttar Pradesh, in fact, of North India as a whole. Note that Agra, which has high negative scores on Components I and IX and high positive scores on Component VIII, is included in Group 8. For more details on KAVAL cities see Ujagir Singh, "KAVAL Towns: A Comparative Study in Functional Aspects of Urban Centers in Uttar Pradesh," The National Geographical Journal of India, VIII (September-December, 1962), 238-49.

[1]It may be pointed out that scores on Components IV, X and I are not uniformly high for all the cities included in this group. This fact renders the interpretation of the group somewhat difficult.

[2]Again, not all cities have high fertility and mortality rates, as shown by the uneven factor scores of these cities on Component X.

[3]For a discussion of some aspects of the Calcutta conurbation, see A. K. Dutt and S. C. Chakraborty, "Reality of Calcutta

other members of the conurbation form a separate group to be mentioned later. These cities have high scores on Components I, II, III, VII and VIII (Table 34). They are characterized by low proportion of female employment, extremely low sex ratios,[1] large proportions of in-migrants from rural areas, very high ratios of workers to population, and very high proportions of workers in manufacturing.[2] These cities have markedly high potentials, resulting from location in the Calcutta conurbation, as is evident from the map (Fig. 6). Furthermore, these cities are marked by small household sizes, relatively low literacy rates, and low rates of population increase (except for Bally) during the past two decades.

TABLE 34

GROUP 7

Cities	Components									
	I	II	III	IV	V	VI	VII	VIII	IX	X
Howrah	-104	200	- 45	-104	78	7	60	-136	19	64
Bally	- 79	194	-192	- 68	- 12	-207	53	-196	- 45	4
Garden Reach	-103	99	-243	- 55	82	20	101	-214	- 37	0
Bhatpara	- 54	85	-272	30	158	- 45	84	-239	- 86	84

Group 8 is a relatively large group containing nine cities --Agra, Saharanpur, Aligarh, Amritsar, Bareilly, Moradabad, Mathura, Shahjahanpur, and Rampur. However, in the 27-group solution,

---

Conurbation," The National Geographical Journal of India, IX (September-December, 1963), 161-74.

[1]Garden Reach has the highest sex ratio (650 females to 1,000 males) in the group. Bally has only 526 females to every 1,000 males.

[2]Bhatpara has 70.8 per cent of the workers engaged in manufacturing. Figures for Bally, Garden Reach and Howrah are 63.5, 56.0 and 43.3 per cent respectively. For further details on these cities see N. R. Kar, "Economic Character of Metropolitan Sphere of Influence of Calcutta," Geographical Review of India, XXV (June, 1963), 108-37. Kar's study, however, is based on data provided by 1951 Census of India.

Rampur joins Gwalior to form a separate group, mainly because they have high (negative) scores on Component X while other members of Group 8 have low (positive) scores on this component (see Table 35).

TABLE 35

GROUP 8

Cities	Components									
	I	II	III	IV	V	VI	VII	VIII	IX	X
Agra	-163	15	11	34	54	105	65	144	- 63	99
Saharanpur	-188	- 8	- 10	- 42	- 20	90	44	108	- 31	38
Aligarh	-152	- 14	- 27	56	15	78	67	42	- 37	3
Amritsar	-185	- 66	42	-117	40	64	37	5	114	55
Bareilly	-151	- 38	34	- 71	18	48	154	16	58	- 98
Moradabad	-178	- 43	- 40	-177	- 38	88	134	98	24	30
Mathura	-122	13	75	- 80	- 82	71	78	77	- 25	65
Shahjahanpur	-137	- 22	98	- 91	-162	132	232	- 23	- 1	54
Rampur	-132	- 13	- 53	- 49	- 74	153	177	47	18	-249

The nine cities of Group 8, with but few exceptions, have high scores on Components I, VI and VII. Accordingly, they are characterized by northern and relatively western location,[1] very low proportions of female workers, low sex ratios,[2] greater accessibility to the railroad network, high degree of clustering,

[1]Note that several of the cities in Group 8 have high scores on Component VIII as well.

[2]Compared with cities in Group 6, these cities have more females per 1,000 males. This may be due to relatively high proportions of female in-migrants in these cities, which in turn may be due to a number of reasons, one of which refers to the in-migration of a large number of Muslim families, particularly women and children, from smaller towns and villages during the post-Partition communal disturbances. See Lal, "Age and Sex Structure of Cities of India," pp. 11, 12.

Related to the above observation is the fact that all these cities have considerably large proportion of Muslim population as compared with other Indian cities which are overwhelmingly non-Muslim.

extremely low literacy rates, low rates of population increase (except for Rampur) during 1941-51, relatively small household sizes, small proportions of in-migrants, low rates of population increase during 1951-61, and relatively large proportions of female in-migrants. Furthermore, these cities have relatively large proportions of in-migrants from other urban centers and a low ratio of workers to total population of the city.

Group 9 consists of five cities of Rajasthan--Jaipur, Ajmer, Jodhpur, Kota, and Bikaner, in addition to three other cities--Jhansi, Bhavnagar, and Burdwan, the last two being at a considerable distance from the rest of the group as well as from each other. Of these cities, Kota and Burdwan form a separate group, according to the 27-group solution.

These cities, in general, have high scores on Components V, IX and to some degree VIII, VII and III (Table 36). Accordingly, they are characterized by low employment in primary industry, very high employment in tertiary industry, large distances to nearest city (100,000 and over),[1] large area, relatively high proportions of in-migrants in the age-group 0-14 years, western location, large proportions of in-migrants from other urban centers, low ratios of workers to population, higher sex ratios than cities in the east, higher female in-migrants, low literacy rates and low rates of population increase during 1941-51 (except for Jaipur).

Group 10 is a regionally compact group of seven cities, six of which are located in the state of Bihar. These cities have high scores on Components II and VIII and a mixture of high and

---

[1]It is interesting to note the difference in the distribution pattern of the two sets of cities, the eastern cities (e.g., cities of the Calcutta conurbation) and the western cities (cities included in Group 9). Whereas the former has a strong tendency toward clustering the latter display a high degree of scatter (see Fig. 6).

low scores on Components IX and X (Table 37). Accordingly, these cities are characterized by northern location, small population sizes, low potentials, large proportions of workers in household industry, relatively large distances between two nearest cities and also to the nearest city over a million population, fewer railroad routes, relatively low proportions of in-migrants, small proportions of workers in manufacturing, relatively eastern location, large proportions of in-migrants from rural areas, moderately high ratios of workers to population, and low sex ratios. In addition, these cities are marked by relatively low fertility and mortality rates, large proportions of in-migrants in the age-group 15 to 34 years and small proportions in the age-group 0-14 years.

TABLE 36

GROUP 9

Cities	Components									
	I	II	III	IV	V	VI	VII	VIII	IX	X
Jaipur	-32	-48	21	68	131	-37	63	123	25	43
Jhansi	-10	-5	67	58	24	-96	132	102	-94	18
Ajmer	-12	-23	129	145	136	11	60	98	-116	-66
Jodhpur	-27	-128	113	202	180	-42	64	17	-106	9
Bhavnagar	2	-90	-3	-24	183	78	-36	87	-109	-37
Bikaner	20	-182	141	34	230	-0	176	78	-61	-144
Kota	67	44	156	317	31	-78	107	3	-173	67
Burdwan	-30	98	186	63	134	39	21	-80	-333	13

TABLE 37

GROUP 10

Cities	Components									
	I	II	III	IV	V	VI	VII	VIII	IX	X
Patna	-23	-41	23	55	-96	-84	13	-113	182	-79
Gorakhpur	-15	-120	21	15	24	-88	59	-137	129	-34
Muzaffarpur	-96	-107	64	1	-75	-47	-61	-165	78	-34
Ranchi	-25	-109	-27	164	-38	-100	-97	-51	44	-56
Gaya	27	-45	11	38	-40	81	100	-125	25	-23
Bhagalpur	-19	-85	-31	18	-7	100	74	-144	31	-146
Darbhanga	-6	-129	-15	-10	-112	18	71	-185	93	-63

Yet another regionally compact group of cities is Group 11 which consists of Ernakulam, Trivandrum, Calicut, and Alleppey--all from the peripherally located state of Kerala. All four are coastal towns, located on the narrow fringe of the Malabar coast. These cities have high scores on Components VI and VII and a mixture of high and low scores on Components VIII and X (Table 38). Accordingly, these cities are characterized by extreme southern location, high sex ratios, high literacy rates, large household sizes, relatively high proportions of telephones and banks, large employment in service industry,[1] low per cent of population increase (except for Ernakulam) during 1951-61, low proportions of in-migrants, and low ratios of workers to population. Other common characteristics of these cities are high proportions of in-migrants from rural areas, and high proportions of female workers. Furthermore, these cities are characterized by small proportions of persons belonging to Scheduled Castes, low accessibility to the railroad network, and long distances to nearest cities over a million and also to other cities of smaller size. The last mentioned measures of relative accessibility appear to be the major factors in differentiating this group from other groups of Indian cities.

TABLE 38

GROUP 11

Cities	Components									
	I	II	III	IV	V	VI	VII	VIII	IX	X
Ernakulam	28	- 71	71	6	- 37	71	-254	- 44	36	-131
Trivandrum	32	- 74	65	54	- 48	140	-265	- 97	73	- 12
Calicut	28	-135	11	12	116	278	-213	- 77	- 11	- 23
Alleppey	122	39	24	9	- 29	276	-217	- 56	- 41	-130

[1]Note that until the merger of the princely states, Trivandrum was the capital of the state of Travancore, and Ernakulam was the capital of Cochin State. At present Trivandrum is the capital of the newly constituted state of Kerala.

Group 12 consists of the five of the most northerly cities of India, namely, Jullundur, Ludhiana, Dehra Dun, Patiala and Meerut. These cities in general have high scores on Components I, V and VIII (Table 39). Accordingly, they are characterized by low sex ratios, low female employment, greater accessibility to the railroad network, short distances to the nearest city over 100,000 population, relatively small proportions of workers in primary industry and high proportions in manufacturing. Furthermore, these cities have low ratios of workers to population and very high proportions of unclassified migrants. The last mentioned factor is so pervasive that it gives a completely distorted picture of the relative distribution of rural and urban in-migrants.[1] In addition, these cities (except for Meerut) show higher literacy rates relative to other northern cities.

TABLE 39

GROUP 12

Cities	Components									
	I	II	III	IV	V	VI	VII	VIII	IX	X
Meerut	-127	- 8	- 19	- 62	- 90	- 29	25	69	40	- 33
Jullundur	-220	- 24	10	- 10	- 41	5	- 61	108	107	6
Ludhiana	-175	- 37	- 52	-129	- 29	- 56	- 83	108	106	- 12
Dehra Dun	-159	6	56	128	- 85	- 36	-207	48	- 55	11
Patiala	-169	- 28	38	40	-121	- 42	- 98	50	10	59

Group 13 is by far the largest group consisting of fourteen cities, nine of which are the coastal towns of Andhra and

[1]The proportion of unclassified in-migrants in these cities are as follows: Meerut (18.90 per cent), Jullundur (55.11 per cent), Ludhiana (50.86 per cent), Dehra Dun (39.12 per cent), and Patiala (39.45 per cent). However, inasmuch as these cities have high negative scores on Component I and positive scores on Component VIII, it is implied that they have relatively small proportion of in-migrants from rural areas and large proportion of in-migrants from other towns.

Madras.[1] According to the 27-group solution, these cities fall into three groups as shown in Table 26. A glance at the factor scores of these cities (Table 40) will show that these three groups are definitely more homogeneous than Group 13 which lumps all the three groups into one group.[2] This difference is worth noting while making a general evaluation of Group 13.

TABLE 40

GROUP 13

Cities	Components									
	I	II	III	IV	V	VI	VII	VIII	IX	X
Tiruchirap-alli	71	35	53	-134	-54	8	-2	69	-34	48
Hubli	66	-33	2	-77	-40	-27	32	86	-17	-84
Amravati	53	12	27	-5	-162	-56	-16	39	41	17
Akola	27	39	86	-110	-146	-31	20	85	42	-30
Raipur	158	83	113	-47	-152	-126	84	-17	49	-136
Vijayawada	114	108	141	-137	-124	-133	22	57	-89	66
Guntur	130	44	-7	-107	-114	-82	60	-25	-37	88
Rajahmundry	112	17	118	-141	-13	1	73	-31	-148	71
Eluru	162	48	55	-106	-137	-35	87	-50	-166	56
Kakinada	69	-4	108	10	-108	7	44	-77	-125	47
Tukicorin	128	31	77	-86	29	159	-104	-126	-151	86
Thanjavur	61	21	41	-31	-162	46	-60	52	-107	104
Nagercoil	85	-58	-2	-72	-140	99	-83	-96	-5	-56
Bandar	43	-35	5	-19	-195	75	-12	-75	-21	52

These cities, in general, have high scores on Components I, IV and V. Accordingly, they are characterized by large female employment, relatively southern location, high sex ratios, very high proportions of female in-migrants, and in-migrants from rural areas, large proportions of workers engaged in primary activity, low employment in manufacturing, short distance by road to nearest

[1] In fact this group contained fifteen cities including Ujjain which was allocated to Group 4 by the discriminant functions analysis, as mentioned before.

[2] Note that Andhra sub-group of cities has very high scores on Components I and IV; the Madras sub-group has high scores on Component V only, and the same is true of a third sub-group of Group 13, namely, Tiruchirapalli, Hubli, Amravati, Akola and Raipur.

city over 100,000 population,[1] relatively small size of population, small area, high density of dwellings per unit area in most of these cities, and small proportions of persons belonging to Scheduled Castes.

Group 14 consists of four cities--Visakhapatnam, Nellore, Cuttack, and Kurnool, the first three being located on the eastern coast of India. These cities have high scores on Components II, VI, and X. Accordingly, they are characterized by high fertility and mortality rates, high proportions of persons belonging to Scheduled Castes, small population sizes, low potentials, low proportions of workers in manufacturing, long distances to nearest city over 100,000 population, high sex ratios (except for Cuttack), relatively large rates of population increase during 1951-61, high ratios of workers to population, relatively high proportions of in-migrants in the age groups 0-14 and 15-34 years, and high proportions of in-migrants from rural areas.[2]

TABLE 41

GROUP 14

Cities	Components									
	I	II	III	IV	V	VI	VII	VIII	IX	X
Visakhapatnam	37	- 76	92	66	- 12	- 95	- 22	- 51	- 39	103
Nellore	48	- 73	- 18	- 47	-120	- 33	- 11	- 36	- 67	178
Kurnool	125	-140	- 33	- 27	- 70	-130	69	- 52	- 29	103
Cuttack	- 82	-212	- 12	141	119	-101	-139	- 87	- 73	125

A glance at the factor scores of these cities shows that on more than one component, Cuttack looks different (as indicated by positive or negative signs) from the rest of the group. No

[1]Note that cities of the Andhra sub-group form a nice cluster in the Krishna-Godavari deltaic region.

[2]Note that these cities have negative (though not very high) scores on Components VIII and IX.

wonder then, that in 27-group solution, it stands out as a separate group (see Table 26).

Group 15 is a small group of only three widely spaced cities not forming a region--Asansol, Jamnagar and Belgaum. These cities have high scores on Components II, IV, and X, and, to a lesser degree, on Components VI and VII (Table 42). These cities have very low fertility and mortality rates, small proportions of persons belonging to Scheduled Castes, large household sizes, small areas, high densities of population and dwellings, low potentials, and relatively small proportions of in-migrants.

TABLE 42

GROUP 15

Cities	Components									
	I	II	III	IV	V	VI	VII	VIII	IX	X
Asansol	-149	- 32	121	-122	37	- 67	- 55	-103	- 34	-203
Jamnagar	- 14	-130	- 18	-110	- 35	- 53	- 40	82	46	-146
Belgaum	24	-125	21	-170	- 94	- 94	- 54	22	51	-146

Group 16 consists of South Suburb, South Dum Dum, Baranagar, and Kamarhati--all of which form part of the Calcutta conurbation. These cities have high scores on Components I, II, VII, IX, II and to a lesser degree, on Components III, VI and X (Table 43). Thus, it would appear that this is one of the most cohesive groups so far as Indian cities are concerned. To mention some of the major similarities, these cities are characterized by low sex ratios, low female employment, and high proportions of unclassified migrants.[1] These cities have high potentials, very small distances to nearest city over 100,000 or a million population (conurbation

[1]The proportion of unclassified in-migrants in these cities are as follows: South Suburb (40.52 per cent), South Dum Dum (61.45 per cent), Baranagar (21.22 per cent) and Kamarhati (26.36 per cent), This factor must have greatly affected the relative distribution of urban and rural in-migrants.

type of distribution pattern), high employment in manufacturing, large proportions of in-migrants, relatively small proportions of female in-migrants, large proportions of in-migrants in the age-group 0-14 years, relatively small population sizes and small areas, low proportions of both banks and telephone connections, high literacy rates, and high rates of population increase during 1941-51 and 1951-61. Some of the other common characteristics of these cities are low fertility and mortality rates, large household sizes (except for Kamarhati), and small proportions of persons belonging to Scheduled Castes.

TABLE 43

GROUP 16

Cities	Components									
	I	II	III	IV	V	VI	VII	VIII	IX	X
South Suburb	-119	149	- 20	18	14	- 59	-137	14	-240	- 97
South Dum Dum	-169	170	- 56	- 24	- 25	- 59	-200	21	-111	-255
Baranagar	-133	127	- 76	-121	73	- 64	-121	- 35	-219	- 33
Kamarhati	- 84	153	-179	- 75	104	-103	- 29	- 66	-181	- 75

Group 17 is a single-member group represented by Kolar Gold Fields, the only major mining city in India.[1] It is characterized obviously by the largest proportion of workers in mining, largest proportions of workers in non-urban functions (primary industry), lowest employment in manufacturing, largest proportion of persons belonging to Scheduled Castes, extremely low densities of population and dwellings per unit area, high sex ratios, small proportions of total in-migrants but very high proportions of female in-migrants. Furthermore, it is the only _city_ of India that lost population during 1951-61.

---

[1]Another major mining town is Dhanbad which is not included in the analysis of Political cities since its population was less than 100,000 in 1961.

TABLE 44

GROUP 17

Cities	Components									
	I	II	III	IV	V	VI	VII	VIII	IX	X
Kolar Gold Fields	- 12	- 5	-325	379	-321	263	33	-145	12	41

Group 18 is another single-member group containing the city of Gauhati. Like Kolar Gold Fields, it has a host of unique properties. It is the easternmost city of India.[1] It has the largest concentration of tertiary activity (especially transport and service functions). It had in 1961 the lowest sex ratio and the lowest potentials (all types of potentials as used in the analysis) of any cities included in the analysis. Gauhati is the first ranking city of India in both the percentage of population increase and the ratio of workers to population. In addition it is marked by extremely remote location (in terms of physical distances to other cities), very high proportions of total in-migrants and in-migrants in the age-group 15-34 years, very high literacy rate and very high mortality rates, especially rate of infant mortality.

TABLE 45

GROUP 18

Cities	Components									
	I	II	III	IV	V	VI	VII	VIII	IX	X
Gauhati	-112	-235	159	5	48	-362	-110	-353	72	226

[1]Note that Shillong which is a few miles east of Gauhati is not included in this analysis because of the size restriction.

The Linkage Tree

Figure 7 shows the "tree" of linkages by which the eighteen groups of 102 Indian cities are combined to form smaller numbers of larger groups. As would appear from the linkage tree, Indian cities, basically, fall into three groups: (1) the Northern cities; (2) the Southern cities and National Metropolises and (3) the Calcutta suburbs,[1] although the cities of Rajasthan and Central India stand apart from the Southern cities until quite late. The Calcutta suburbs consist of only eight cities while the Northern and Southern groups contain 35 and 59 cities respectively. It is important to note some of the major differences among these broad groups of Indian cities.

Calcutta suburbs are dominated by manufacturing. They are characterized by highly unbalanced sex ratios, low female employment, relatively high ratios of workers to population, high degrees of clustering, high potentials, and relatively large proportions of in-migrants.

The Northern cities (i.e., Groups 6, 8, 10, 12, 14, and 15) are characterized by small female employment, low sex ratios,[2] low literacy rates, relatively large proportions of persons belonging to Scheduled Castes, and greater accessibility to the railroad network. Furthermore, these cities have small proportions of in-migrants, low ratios of workers to population, and fewer banks as compared with Southern cities. In general, these cities showed relatively small rates of population change (in-

---

[1]Significantly enough, Calcutta suburbs (Groups 7 and 16 in Fig. 7) maintain their identity as a separate group till the end of the stepwise grouping, even after the Northern and Southern cities have merged into one group.

[2]Both female employment and sex ratio, however, are not as low as in the case of Calcutta suburbs.

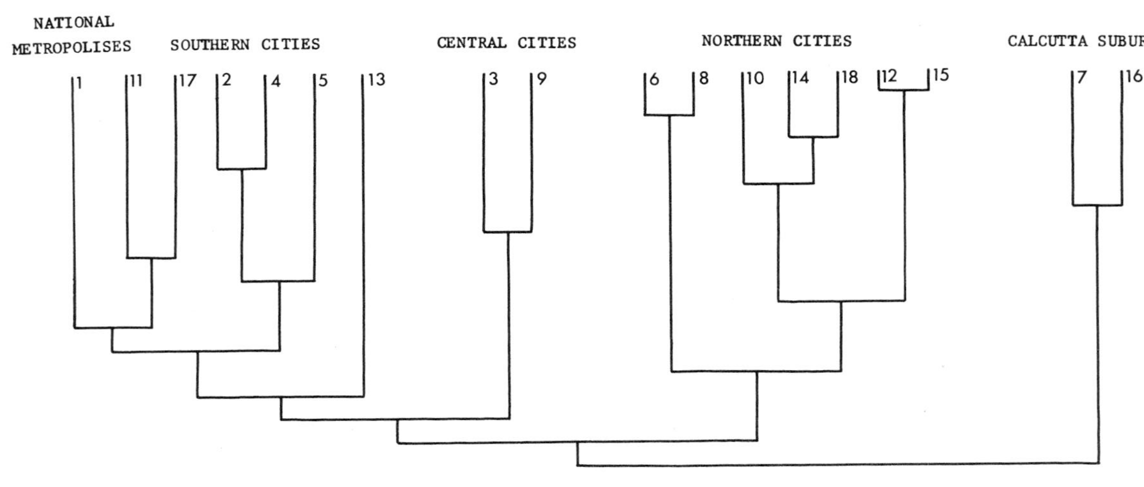

Fig. 7. -- Indian Cities (Political), The Linkage Tree, Based on 62 Variables

crease) during the past two census decades, 1941-51 and 1951-61.[1]

The Southern cities, on the other hand, are characterized by greater female employment, more balanced sex ratios, larger proportions of female in-migrants and in-migrants from rural areas, higher literacy rates, greater number of banks per unit of population, lower proportions of persons belonging to the Scheduled Castes, lower accessibility to railroad network, relatively large rates of population change (increase) during 1941-61, especially, 1941-51, and higher proportion of in-migrants, as compared with Northern cities.

At one stage in the stepwise grouping, the Southern cities split into three groups:[2] (1) the cities of Rajasthan and a few other cities (Bhopal, Jabalpur, Nagpur, Warangal, and Hyderabad) which have a somewhat central location in India (Groups 3 and 9 on the linkage tree); (2) the cities of Madras and Andhra Littoral together with a few other cities (Group 13, see Fig. 7); (3) the balance of the 59 Southern cities, almost all of which have western location relative to cities included in Group 13. These cities are represented by Groups 11, 17, 2, 4 and 5 in the order given on the

---

[1]It may be noted that the various characteristics of the Northern cities as described here have a relative value. In each case, the Northern cities are compared with cities which have relatively southern location.

[2]It is interesting to note that the boundary lines separating the various constituent groups of the Southern cities have a well-marked longitudinal (North-South) orientation, a factor that helps in identifying the three sub-groups.

The only exception is the line separating Rajasthan cities of Group 9 from other Southern cities, which runs East-West rather than North-South. This exception is significant to the extent that the cities of Rajasthan display certain characteristics which are not shared by other Southern cities. For example, these cities have very low scores, and in many cases even negative scores, on Component I, negative scores on Component II, and high positive scores on Component III, the latter implying a heavy concentration of tertiary activity. Note that until recently these Rajasthan cities were capitals of one or the other of the princely states in this region.

linkage tree (Fig. 7). In addition, the national metropolises, with their more balanced occupational structure, continued growth, etc. are put into the same major cluster of Southern cities.[1]

The differences between these groups will become apparent when, in later sections, we will discuss the differentiating properties of the various constituent sub-groups of each one of the three broad groups.

Calcutta Suburbs

At the eighteen group level, the Calcutta suburbs are differentiated into two Groups, 7 and 16 (Table 26). Group 7 contains Howrah, Bally, Garden Reach and Bhatpara, while Group 16 consists of South Suburb, South Dum Dum, Baranagar and Kamarhati. Note the factor scores of these two groups of cities on Components I to X (see Tables 34 and 43). While Group 7 has high scores on Component III, positive scores on Components VII and high negative scores on Component VIII, Group 16 has low scores on Component III, negative scores on Component IX and to a lesser degree on Component X. Thus, cities of Group 7 have relatively larger employment in manufacturing, lower literacy rates, smaller rates of population increase during 1941-61, smaller household sizes, higher proportions of in-migrants from rural areas and much higher ratios of workers to population and lower sex ratios than cities in Group 16.

Northern Cities

Briefly, the differentiating properties of the seven groups of Northern cities are as follows:

---

[1]It may be difficult, in the first glance, to explain the inclusion of Group 1 in the category of Southern cities but a little probe into the factor scores of Group 1 would reveal that as a group the three national metropolises of India are, in many ways, more akin to Southern cities than cities with a relative Northern or North-eastern location.

Group 6 consists of cities which are all very important railway junctions. Also, these cities are characterized by relatively low density of population and of dwellings per unit area as they all occupy relatively large areas.

Group 8 consists of cities which form a neat cluster in the northwestern part of Uttar Pradesh. Most of the cities in this group are marked by relatively high densities of population and of dwellings per unit area, smaller percentages of persons belonging to Scheduled Castes, and greater degrees of clustering than in any other group of the Northern cities. In many other respects, however, as apparent from the factor scores, Groups 6 and 8 seem to have considerable similarity. This fact is borne out in the linkage tree where Group 8 initially joins Group 6.

Group 10 contains cities which are characterized by eastern location, high proportions of in-migrants from rural areas, relatively high ratios of workers to population, and large household sizes.

Group 12 comprises cities of the northwest. They are differentiated from other Northern cities by higher literacy rates (except for Meerut), higher ratios of telephone connections and banks per capita, and very high percentages of unclassified in-migrants.

One seemingly odd group in the Northern branch of the linkage tree is Group 14, which consists of four cities, three of which have southern location, large female employment, and large proportions of in-migrants from rural areas. How is it, then, that it is included in the groups of Northern cities as shown on the linkage tree? The probable explanation is that, although Group 14 does not have some of those properties which characterize the Northern cities, it certainly has considerable affinity with cities which have relative eastern (more appropriately northeastern) location. The linkage tree lends support to this explanation. As the process of grouping advances Group 18 joins Group 14, and at a later stage the two together combine with Group 10 which also has definite northeastern location.

Group 15 is a small group of three cities which show very low fertility and mortality rates and low proportions of persons belonging to Scheduled Castes, small area, and therefore high densities of population and of dwellings per unit area.

Group 18 is a single-member group represented by Gauhati which, as mentioned in the previous section, is definitely a unique city of India.

Southern Cities

The Southern cities, at the 18-group level, are distributed into nine groups, 1, 2, 3, 4, 5, 9, 11, 13 and 17. The differentiating properties of each one of these nine groups are outlined as follows:

Group 1 consists of the three national metropolises of India, Bombay, Delhi, and Calcutta--all of which typically represent the large city with definite metropolitan functions.

Group 2 is distinguished from other groups inasmuch as all the five cities of the group have relatively high fertility and mortality rates.

Group 3 is characterized by relatively low (lower than in any other group) fertility and mortality rates, large proportions of in-migrants from rural areas and relatively high female employment. The last two characteristics, however, are shared by other groups (Groups 5 and 13) too.

Group 4 is not a very homogeneous group as is evident from the factor scores of cities included in this group. In fact, it consists of two distinct groups according to the 27-group solution, as mentioned before. However, at the 18-group level, it differs from other groups in terms of its large rate of population increase during 1941-51 and high proportion of in-migrants from urban areas.[1]

Group 5 contains cities which are among the important manufacturing centers of India. They have a very high proportion of their total labor force concentrated in manufacturing and household industry. It is worth mentioning that these industrial centers are quite different from their counterparts, the Calcutta suburbs, in terms of sex ratios, female employment, relative accessibility, and density of population and of dwellings per unit area.

Group 9 consists of cities which with the exception of Bhavnagar have much larger proportions of workers engaged in tertiary activity than other Southern cities.

Group 11 has very high negative scores on Component VII and high positive scores on Component VI. Accordingly, some of the distinctive features of this group of cities are extreme southern location, large household size, high literacy rate, very low ratio of workers to population, very low proportion of in-migrants, and large proportion of banks and telephone connections.

As mentioned in the previous section, Group 13 is a relatively loose group of sixteen cities characterized in particular by very high proportion of female in-migrants and in-migrants from rural areas, relatively small population size and area, and very high proportion of labor force engaged in primary activity.

Finally, Group 17 is a single member group represented

---

[1]Note that the Southern cities have relatively large proportion of in-migrants from rural areas.

by the well-known mining center of Kolar Gold Fields. Like Gauhati, this too is a unique city as mentioned in the previous section. No further comments are needed to justify its separate identity as a single-member group.

A Second Analysis of Political Cities

From the account in the previous section it would appear that Groups 2, 3, 14, and 15 and to a lesser degree, Groups 6 and 8 owe their separate identity because the cities included in these groups have either very high or very low fertility and mortality rates as revealed by their scores (positive or negative) on the tenth component.[1] It would be interesting to note the changes that would emerge in the factor structure and the resulting groupings if the four variables relating to fertility and mortality rates were deleted. Accordingly, a separate components analysis was run using fifty-eight variables instead of sixty-two as in the first analysis. The results of the components analysis are given in Table 46.

As expected, the basic factor structure remained unaltered. The only noticeable change is a shift in the relative importance of the various components. Of particular interest is the fifth component, identified as size of population, which in this analysis explains 7.2 per cent of the total variance as compared with 5.3 as in the first analysis (Table 13). Another component which is affected is the sixth component of the first analysis. This component is split between Components IX and X of the second analysis (Table 46).

---

[1]In fact there are more than six groups of cities which have high scores on the tenth component, but these six groups are differentiated from other groups only on the basis of their ratings on the tenth component.

TABLE 46

INDIAN CITIES (POLITICAL)[a]
MAJOR DIMENSIONS OF VARIATION
(PERCENTAGE OF VARIANCE EXPLAINED BY EACH COMPONENT)

	Components	Per Cent of Variance Explained by Each Component
I.	North-south regional differentiation by sex	15.8
II.	Conurbations and accessibility	10.1
III.	Commercial/industrial structure	7.8
IV.	Rural orientation	7.4
V.	Size of population	7.2
VI.	Compactness	6.6
VII.	North-south regional differentiation of literacy, urban services and population change, 1941-51	6.0
VIII.	East-west regional differentiation of migration characteristics and ratio of workers to population	5.3
IX.	Population change between 1951 and 1961	4.6
X.	Migration characteristics	4.5
Total percentage of variance accounted for by Components I to X		75.3

[a]This analysis is based on fifty-eight variables.

These changes in the factor structure have affected the pattern of groupings as shown in Fig. 8.[1] Obviously the groups that had high scores (positive or negative) on the tenth component in the first analysis are altered most. Group 2 now consists of only two cities--Madras and Hyderabad, both million-cities ranking respectively fourth and fifth in terms of size of population. Group 3 in this analysis consists of cities which in the first

[1]Note that Fig. 8 represents 20-group solution, three of which (Calcutta, Kolar Gold Fields and Gauhati) are the single-member groups.

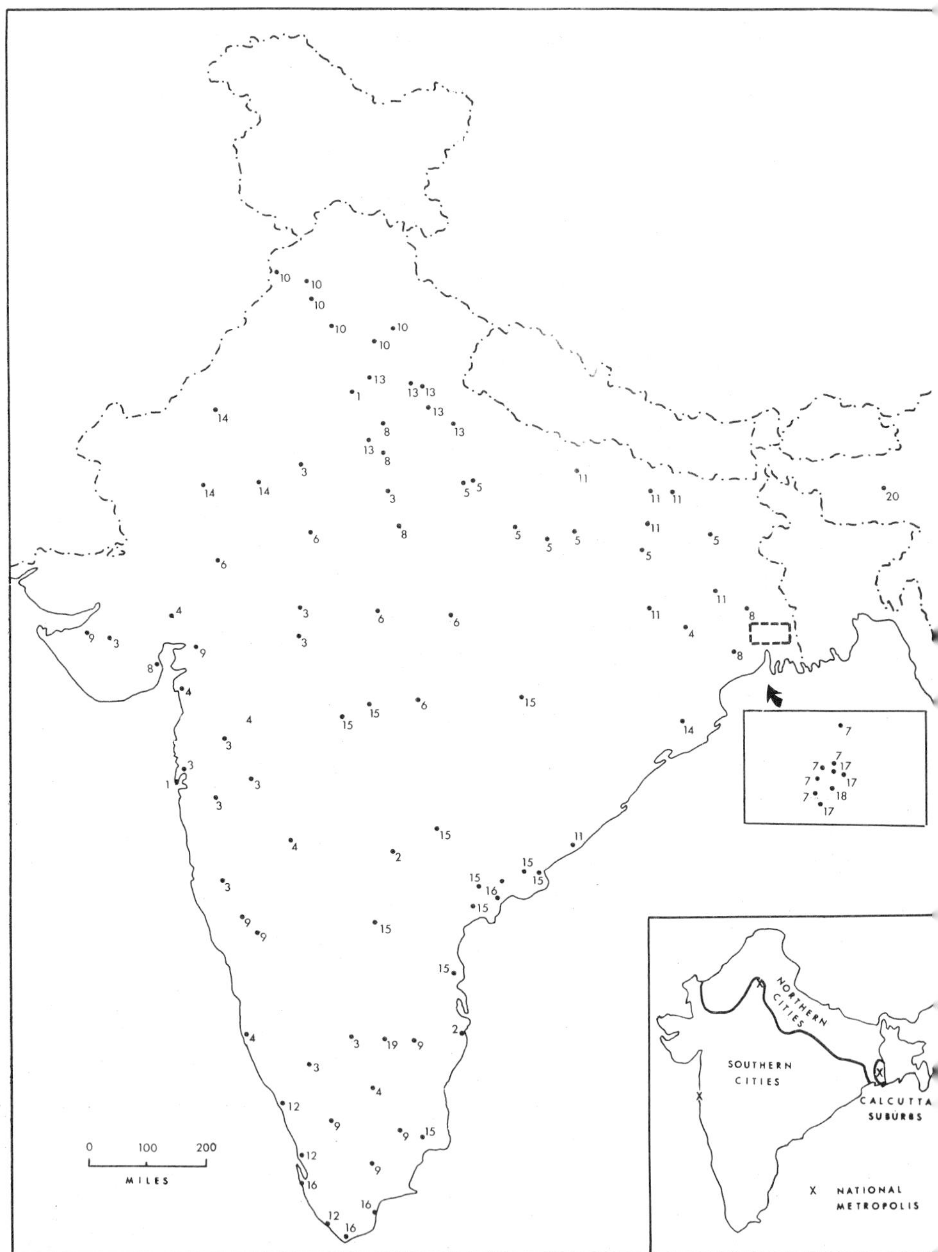

Fig. 8. -- Indian Cities (Political), A Multivariate Classification Based on 58 Variables

analysis (see Fig. 6) formed part of Groups 4 and 9. Groups 14 and 15 have completely disappeared in the form they appeared in Fig. 6. Groups 6 and 10 of the first analysis appear as Groups 5 and 11 but with a markedly different structure. Changes pertaining to a few other groups are also noticeable (Fig. 8) but those are not too radical.

The linkage tree (Fig. 9) of these twenty groups shows clearly the three major groups of 102 Indian cities: (1) the Northern cities; (2) the Southern cities; and (3) the Calcutta suburbs. However, the Calcutta suburbs in this analysis seem to have greater affinity to the Northern cities (Fig. 9) as compared with their counterparts in Fig. 7.

Results of Grouping the Town-Groups

As already mentioned in Chapter II, the component analysis of 102 town-groups and 53 variables produced a factor structure which was in no way markedly different from that obtained for the 102 political cities (see Tables 13 and 14). However, one interesting change was noted in the structure of second component (conurbations and accessibility) which, in the town-group analysis, shows much higher correlations with the size of population and also with the three variables of potentials of population. This and a few other relatively minor changes basically relate to the very definition of a town-group which obviously is greater in size than the political city, as it includes other municipal and non-municipal areas too.

As long as there is some difference in the factor structure of these two units of observation, political cities and the town-groups, it would be interesting to determine the pattern of similarity that emerges as a result of the grouping of town-groups. The results of the stepwise grouping of 102 town-groups are re-

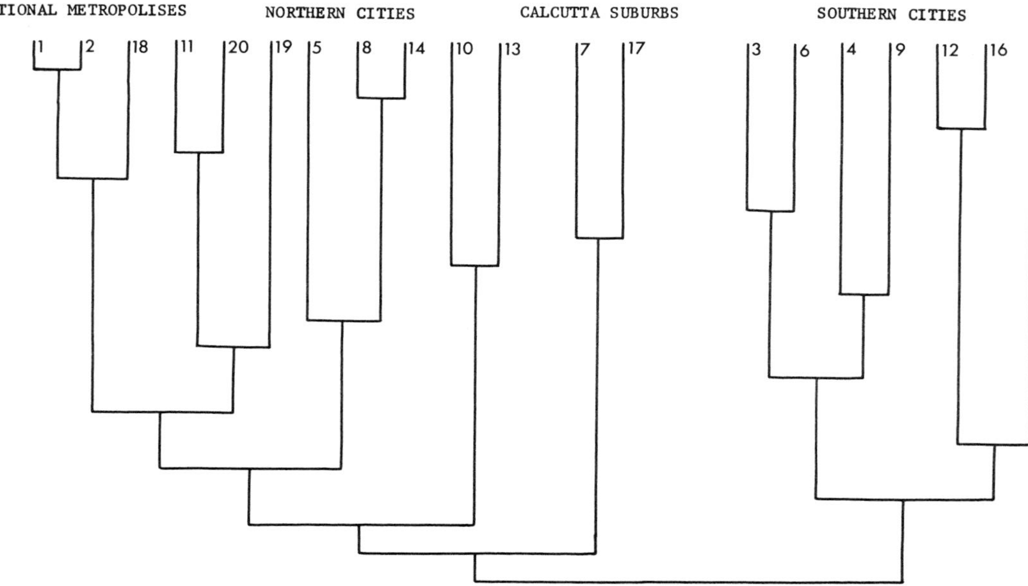

Fig. 9. -- Indian Cities (Political), The Linkage Tree, Based on 58 Variables

ported in Table 47 which also contains the factor scores of each town-group on Components I to X.[1] The distribution of the nineteen groups is shown in Figure 11.

TABLE 47

INDIAN TOWN GROUPS
A MULTIFACTOR CLASSIFICATION INTO NINETEEN GROUPS

Groups of Cities	Components									
	I	II	III	IV	V	VI	VII	VIII	IX	X
Group 1										
Bombay	6	412	27	-86	186	-57	-53	40	-8	-49
Calcutta	-62	425	135	-7	-50	-357	-47	81	-59	-18
Delhi	-67	295	19	89	50	-199	-4	6	23	19
Group 2										
Madras	24	216	92	125	99	31	41	52	-72	181
Hyderabad	179	168	41	159	-50	-33	92	-9	-49	-90
Visakhapatnam	58	-76	19	137	59	1	22	-100	-147	64
Burdwan	-58	15	87	108	64	104	-30	-84	-100	-76
Group 3										
Bangalore	62	161	-150	-39	38	33	32	-90	-10	99
Nasik	30	55	-175	-10	134	124	64	-44	-16	56
Kanpur	-141	148	-93	-71	-2	10	-21	-105	-128	107
Dhanbad	-132	6	-306	-168	183	-4	-100	-5	-169	-114
Group 4										
Ahmedabad	-18	149	131	-158	15	-81	110	44	-2	43
Sholapur	103	-8	139	-233	-92	30	168	98	-32	25
Surat	56	-9	237	-163	26	68	161	109	-63	107
Jamshedpur	-28	-3	16	-221	101	59	128	-15	-130	-147
Malegaon	69	-95	57	-466	-49	62	98	48	-29	-16
Group 5										
Poona	78	123	-23	49	145	95	88	-13	16	-38
Mysore	52	16	-9	80	27	148	55	38	16	2
Ahmednagar	72	-5	-3	-9	76	92	90	84	-29	-20
Baroda	-16	10	117	-41	77	104	66	34	43	13
Bhavnagar	-5	-36	120	9	33	131	144	-4	57	-34
Rajkot	-1	-38	29	11	88	124	36	-46	100	11
Group 6										
Nagpur	129	128	-37	-67	-9	-61	65	-135	38	-9
Jabalpur	28	59	-96	-54	-44	-133	133	-51	-4	-97
Bhopal	-35	12	-77	-72	-26	-66	96	-222	88	-90
Mangalore	162	-55	-42	-94	45	-76	147	30	187	-57
Warangal	162	-6	-97	-59	-84	81	29	-23	-78	-132
Sagar	35	-37	-145	-149	-147	-93	140	67	-11	-52

[1]The optimality of these groups was tested using multiple discriminant analysis. The results showed one change. Jamnagar which is included in Group 14 was reallocated to Group 5.

TABLE 47.--Continued

Groups of Cities	Components									
	I	II	III	IV	V	VI	VII	VIII	IX	X
Group 7										
Lucknow	-105	127	23	54	- 69	- 61	- 15	- 7	- 11	1
Allahabad	- 54	54	- 1	85	- 60	- 75	- 2	10	- 62	- 23
Gwalior	- 39	58	- 58	- 28	- 84	52	23	2	- 12	- 85
Jhansi	- 35	11	- 24	67	- 81	19	78	- 65	- 66	- 30
Patna	- 26	22	- 45	74	15	- 80	- 28	80	- 55	- 87
Gorakhpur	- 63	- 58	29	- 1	- 47	-139	60	28	6	- 70
Muzaffarpur	-122	-106	6	68	40	- 91	- 41	85	21	- 59
Gaya	13	- 31	- 13	26	-103	- 36	- 2	18	- 50	- 36
Darbhanga	- 3	- 94	- 26	21	-123	- 65	- 43	123	- 44	- 23
Bhagalpur	- 37	- 72	1	- 36	- 88	- 22	- 8	106	- 52	-118
Monghyr-Jamal-pur	1	- 57	- 22	- 87	- 83	- 25	- 26	194	- 43	-265
Rampur	-120	- 19	17	- 43	-189	112	-177	55	45	-172
Group 8										
Agra	-159	93	12	21	-119	74	6	54	1	104
Aligarh	-130	15	17	2	-102	116	12	45	- 51	7
Mathura	-117	6	12	96	- 44	106	- 64	- 25	- 29	69
Meerut	-147	41	- 41	20	- 20	109	3	46	51	- 14
Jullundur	-209	8	- 22	20	49	40	- 2	35	84	42
Ambala	-171	- 10	- 60	69	56	62	- 73	- 2	32	44
Patiala	-161	- 63	- 76	51	32	71	- 71	- 72	139	98
Amritsar	-185	- 20	124	- 10	-187	- 91	18	- 12	145	70
Bareilly	-154	- 1	51	16	-159	33	- 22	- 34	62	- 74
Ludhiana	-167	- 36	111	-120	16	12	- 55	68	144	14
Moradabad	-162	- 30	144	- 56	-132	93	-180	38	19	57
Saharanpur	-187	- 21	61	- 36	- 68	105	- 54	2	46	48
Group 9										
Varanasi	- 50	57	29	- 35	-173	-144	- 20	42	- 77	114
Mirzapur	17	- 18	- 15	33	-214	-124	- 57	- 3	- 76	33
Shahjahanpur	-113	- 21	- 8	91	-309	- 20	-109	7	28	85
Group 10										
Madurai	108	11	198	- 1	28	- 10	27	29	11	135
Coimbatore	79	1	109	- 28	126	8	39	- 19	27	151
Indore	- 33	54	26	- 53	27	48	- 1	- 30	- 39	215
Vellore	77	- 49	39	- 11	9	95	3	8	- 19	227
Nellore	73	- 97	12	43	5	64	- 28	- 12	- 65	169
Salem	130	- 20	109	-143	- 63	18	43	31	- 38	149
Kurnool	125	-106	- 1	- 20	- 72	13	86	- 17	- 83	109
Group 11										
Jaipur	- 49	24	45	34	- 32	82	141	-176	- 16	76
Jodhpur	- 42	- 43	- 39	144	- 47	45	201	-211	- 21	14
Ajmer	30	11	37	169	- 45	87	137	-121	- 66	-111
Udaipur	61	- 43	- 20	87	- 20	- 18	157	-136	4	-137
Kota	- 12	- 11	-221	100	- 49	- 12	133	-329	35	13
Bikaner	18	- 67	102	140	-260	- 67	249	-133	128	-146

TABLE 47.--Continued

Groups of Cities	Components									
	I	II	III	IV	V	VI	VII	VIII	IX	X
Group 12										
Cochin	57	19	-51	130	137	-54	53	105	224	-64
Alleppey	99	-1	-85	10	130	-23	-38	158	268	-40
Trivandrum	78	25	-145	133	74	-88	36	215	88	96
Calicut	3	-25	-78	27	93	38	129	131	208	103
Group 13										
Tiruchirapalli	107	-7	122	47	29	29	-122	-39	20	38
Vijayawada	126	-12	130	79	61	1	-225	-133	-21	-6
Rajahmundry	139	-71	196	75	-19	9	-111	-42	-122	5
Guntur	102	-30	59	-66	-16	-27	-177	-92	-4	60
Eluru	163	-79	53	-8	-32	-4	-157	-33	-62	25
Ujjain	30	1	47	-31	-2	34	-69	-57	-54	23
Tuticorin	122	-72	7	11	142	8	-128	-105	48	52
Raipur	152	-36	18	21	8	-142	-208	-115	-33	-164
Kakinada	103	-68	7	125	-39	3	-105	-49	-73	14
Thanjavur	117	-51	-28	84	5	20	-132	13	36	121
Bandar	87	-81	-30	50	-34	-7	-98	61	-31	40
Group 14										
Hubli	66	-9	-18	12	-40	-3	-12	20	118	-69
Akola	44	-8	40	57	-18	-37	-104	-30	121	-35
Amra ati	64	-16	-61	38	-10	-28	-42	-62	92	20
Jamnagar	11	-107	69	8	37	71	3	34	110	-95
Belgaum	43	-68	33	39	20	-45	-27	101	148	-87
Kolhapur	6	-23	-117	-25	27	1	-43	74	142	5
Sangli	52	-5	-184	-38	-46	-33	-106	-1	169	4
Palayamcottai	132	-23	-104	-73	-83	-125	-119	60	101	63
Nagercoil	63	-94	-71	-37	-31	-108	-85	81	251	31
Group 15										
Kalyan	29	70	89	-50	218	195	-229	-61	15	-136
Asansol	-159	-20	72	-102	140	37	-96	-13	-12	-227
Kharagpur	12	8	140	38	80	146	-33	-18	-170	-365
Group 16										
Dehra Dun	-143	-33	-97	114	167	88	33	79	-2	-24
Ranchi	-24	-49	-110	51	135	34	99	71	-127	-84
Cuttack	-131	-104	-56	5	73	-53	171	111	-12	95
Group 17										
Shillong	10	-220	23	161	192	-315	1	212	-323	-42
Gauhati	-243	-334	86	20	225	-305	122	-27	-155	151
Group 18										
Kolar Gold Fields	122	71	-392	9	-163	259	-72	263	-339	118
Group 19										
Durg	-58	-87	-175	-328	96	-206	-158	-400	-48	83

KEY TO FIGURE 10

1. Amritsar*
2. Jullundur*
3. Ludhiana
4. Patiala
5. Ambala*
6. Saharanpur
7. Delhi*
8. Meerut*
9. Moradabad*
10. Rampur
11. Bareilly*
12. Bikaner
13. Aligarh
14. Shahjahanpur*
15. Mathura*
16. Agra*
17. Jodhpur
18. Ajmer
19. Jaipur
20. Gwalior
21. Kanpur*
22. Lucknow*
23. Gorakhpur
24. Muzaffarpur
25. Darbhanga
26. Udaipur
27. Dehra Dun*
28. Kota
29. Jhansi*
30. Allahabad*
31. Mirzapur
32. Varanasi*
33. Gaya
34. Patna
35. Monghyr-Jamalpur*
36. Bhagalpur
37. Jamnagar
38. Rajkot
39. Bhavnagar
40. Ahmedabad*
41. Baroda
42. Indore
43. Ujjain
44. Bhopal*
45. Sagar*
46. Jabalpur*
47. Ranchi*
48. Dhanbad*
49. Asansol*
50. Jamshedpur*
51. Burdwan
52. Kharagpur
53. Calcutta*
54. Surat
55. Ahmednagar
56. Nasik*
57. Nalegaon
58. Akola
59. Amravati
60. Nagpur*
61. Durg*
62. Raipur
63. Cuttack
64. Poona*
65. Kolhapur*
66. Sangli*
67. Sholapur
68. Hyderabad*
69. Warangal
70. Visakhapatnam
71. Belgaum*
72. Hubli-Dharwar*
73. Kurnool
74. Guntur
75. Vijayawada
76. Bombay*
77. Bandar
78. Eluru
79. Kalyan*
80. Rajahmundry
81. Kakinada
82. Nellore
83. Mangalore*
84. Mysore
85. Bangalore*
86. Kolar Gold Fields
87. Vellore*
88. Madras
89. Calicut*
90. Coimbatore
91. Salem
92. Tiruchirapalli
93. Thanjavur
94. Cochin*
95. Alleppey
96. Trivandrum*
97. Nagercoil
98. Palayamcottai*
99. Tuticorin*
100. Madurai
101. Gauhati
102. Shillong*

* Town-Group

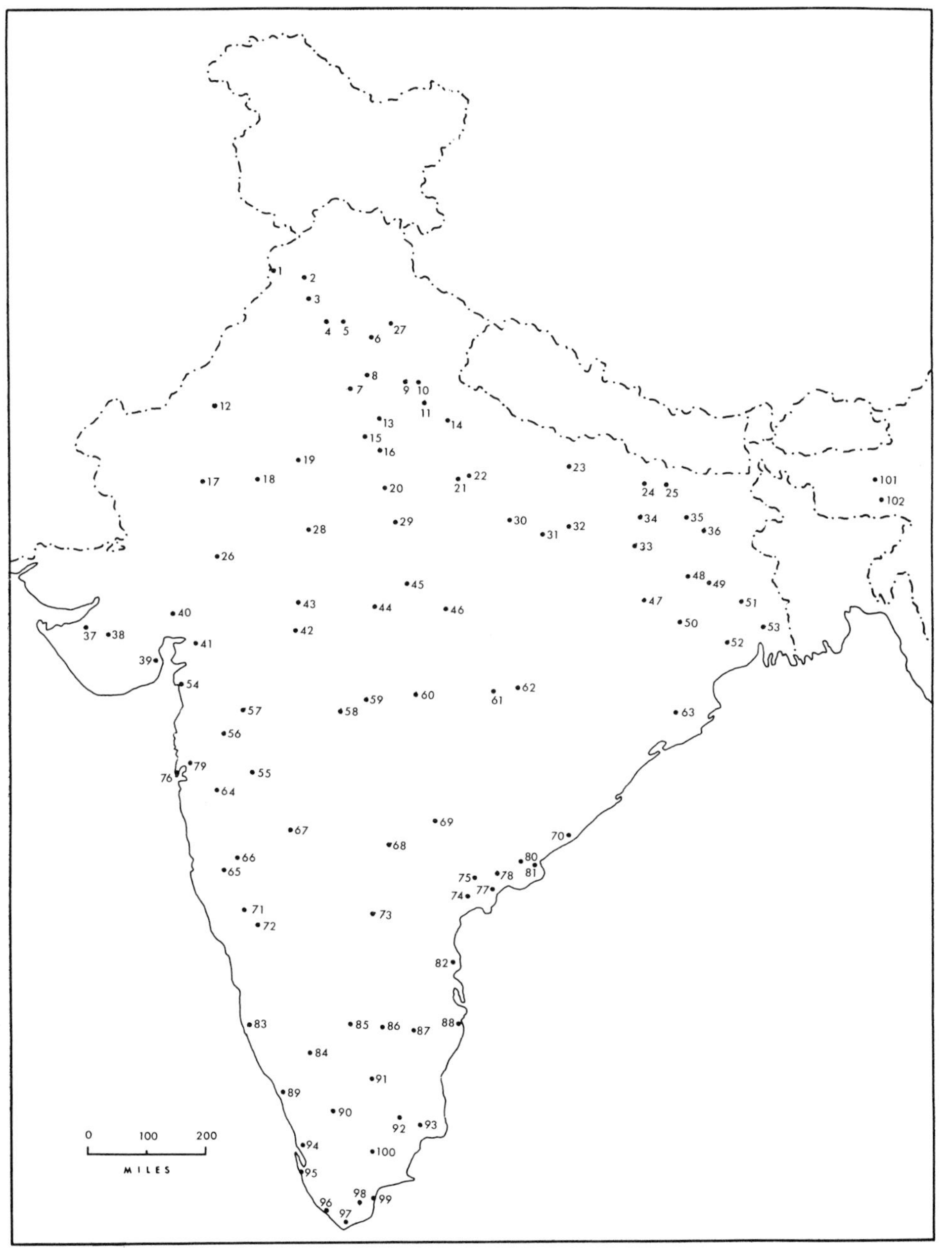

Fig. 10. -- Location of Indian Town-Groups, 1961

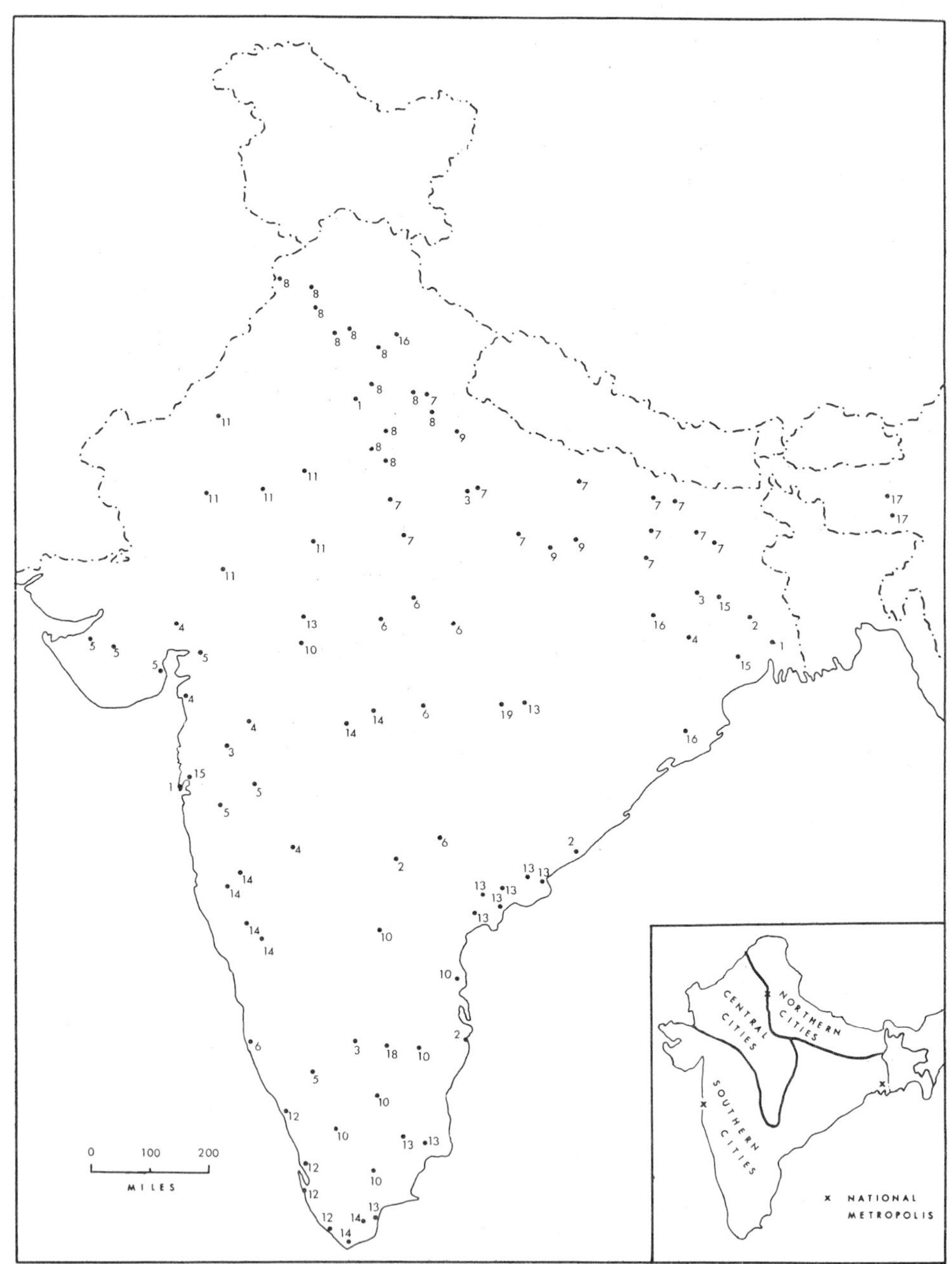

Fig. 11. -- Indian Town-Groups, A Multivariate Classification Based on 53 Variables

A comparison of Figs. 6 and 11 would reveal that no major differences exist in the group structure of the two units of observation, political cities and town-groups. Some of the more obvious though minor differences in the two group structures relate to Groups 2, 4 and 13 as they appear in Fig. 6. Group 2 in the case of town-groups consists of Madras, Hyderabad, Visakhapatnam and Burdwan, all of which have relatively large concentration of tertiary activity, relative eastern location and large proportions of persons belonging to Scheduled Castes. Group 4 of political cities is divided between Groups 3 and 5 of town-groups (Fig. 11). Group 13 of political cities is split between Groups 13 and 14 of town-groups. In addition, Groups 7 and 16 of political cities appear as Group 2 (town-group of Calcutta) in Fig. 11.[1] Group 19 consists of the town-group of Durg (containing the steel town of Bhilainagar) which is the only steel town of India with a population greater than 100,000.

The basic pattern of grouping of 102 town-groups is revealed in the linkage tree (Fig. 12). A comparison of Figs. 7 and 12 shows that the basic pattern of grouping remains the same in both the cases. Like the political cities, town-groups basically fall into two broad groups: (1) the Northern cities and (2) the Southern cities. Also, groups of cities with a somewhat central location (Groups 6 and 11 in Figure 11) form sub-groups of the broader group of the Southern cities.[2] The town-group of Calcutta

[1]Note that the town-group of Calcutta as defined here includes not only eight _cities_ of the Calcutta conurbation (cities over 100,000 population) but also several other urban centers of smaller size. For further details see Appendix A.

[2]It can be seen in the linkage tree that at one level in the stepwise grouping there are in fact five major groups of 102 town-groups: (1) Unique cities (Groups 1, 17 and 19); (2) the Southern cities; (3) the Central cities; (4) the Coastal cities (both east and west coasts); and (5) the Northern cities.

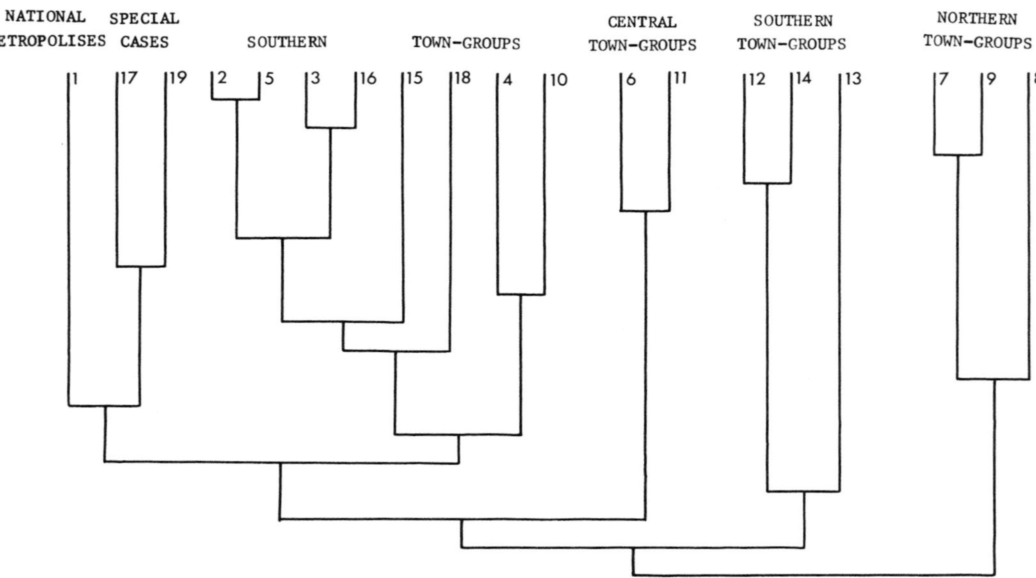

Fig. 12. -- Indian Town-Groups, The Linkage Tree, Based on 53 Variables

of course does not stand out as a separate major group as did the two groups of cities in the Calcutta Conurbation (Groups 7 and 16 in Fig. 7); rather, it links with the other metropolitan town-groups. It should be realized that in the case of town-groups, the regional differentiation, particularly the east-west differentiation is not quite as prominent as was the case with political cities. This is clear from the factor structure of these two units of observation (See Tables 13 and 14).

CHAPTER IV

IMPLICATIONS

The purpose of this investigation was to identify the critical properties of Indian cities that together constitute a system. More specifically, an attempt was made to discover the dimensions of variation along which Indian cities are arrayed--in short, to describe the _state_ of the system. Let us review briefly the major findings of the enquiry.

Dimensions of Variation

One of the major research findings is the discovery that over 70 per cent of the variance of 102 Indian cities on sixty-two variables (whether the cities are defined as political cities or town-groups) is accounted for by only ten dimensions. Three separate analyses--one with political cities and sixty-two variables, the second with political cities and fifty-eight variables and the third with town-groups and fifty-three variables--yielded almost the same set of components (see Tables 13, 14 and 46). This indicates some consistency in the components which, as noted before, are composite statements of the way Indian cities differ from each other.

What are these dimensions of variation of Indian cities? Indian cities differ from each other in terms of (1) a north-south regionalism based on female labor force and sex ratio, (2) generalized accessibility and clustering, (3) compactness, (4) occupational structure (commercial versus industrial), (5) rural orientation, (6) city size, (7) population change (8) east-west regionalism based on occupational and migration characteristics,sex ratio and degree of clustering. Together the ten dimensions summarize the story of Indian urbanization as told by the sixty-two variables, at least 70 per cent of it.

At this stage a comparison of the dimensions of variation of Indian cities with those found both for Western and for other non-Western cities will help illuminate the differences between Indian and other patterns of urbanization.[1]

As examples of Western cities, we have the results of components analyses of the cities of Britain and the United States.[2] In the case of the British towns,[3] the four principal components that explain about 60 per cent of the total variance are social class, population change between 1931 and 1951 and that between 1951 and 1958, and, finally, overcrowding. In the case of United States cities, the first four factors that explain about 63 per cent of the total variance are size, population change, social status (income, education, etc.), and functional differentiation.

One example for non-Western cities is provided by Forrest Pitts who made a study of Korean business centers (seventy-seven cities and towns of all sizes), within the framework of factor

---

[1]It need be mentioned that this comparison is bound to be highly generalized and crude since each study utilizes a different set of variables.

[2]See Moser and Scott, <u>op. cit</u>., p. 14 and also pp. 71-73; Harold H. Mayer of the University of Chicago has recently completed a study of United States cities using factor analysis.

[3]In the case of British towns it is the central city which forms the unit of observation, as opposed to standard metropolitan statistical areas (SMSA's) in the case of United States cities. Also, British towns study does not have variables of spatial interest which are included in the study of the United States cities. Both studies utilize relatively much more refined and also more varied set of variables than used in the case of non-Western cities.

analysis.[1] His first five factors are size,[2] light manufacture and wholesaling, agricultural servicing, supplying for primary production enterprises, and a primary processing and crafts factor.[3]

Granting that each study utilizes a set of variables which often are very much different from those of the other, and this renders any comparison of the results extremely difficult, one generalization can still be made. It seems that five factors--size, the specific set of economic specialties, population change, density, and some social characteristics such as income and literacy, are sure to emerge as independent differentiating elements of urban systems in any situation, Western or non-Western, unless the variables related to these factors are omitted. It also is interesting to note that in the case of both Korea and India a factor of rural orientation is produced, whereas such a dimension did not exist in the Western cases.

It is not surprising that the factor of population size appears in almost all the cases under review. The sociological significance of "size" has been stressed quite often in the literature.[4] City-size or "the size of community," according to Duncan, "is closely connected with whatever it is that produces a

---

[1]Forrest R. Pitts, "Korean Business Centers Study," A Technical Report to the Western Management Science Institute, University of California, Los Angeles, December 31, 1963. (Mimeographed.) This study utilizes an extremely large number of variables (258), mostly business types or central services.

[2]Later on, the name was changed by the author, to "intellectual orientation and middle-class dominance."

[3]Pitts has not included variables of spatial or demographic interest except for population of the city.

[4]See Amos Hawley, Human Ecology (New York: Roland Press Company, 1950), pp. 122-23; Duncan, Metropolis and Region, pp. 23-81; Leo F. Schnore and David Varley, "Some Concommitants of Metropolitan Size," American Sociological Review, XX (August, 1955), 408-14.

hierarchy."[1] City-size seems to play a significant role in India's urban system as well. The size factor emerges in all the three components analyses of Indian cities. An idea of its importance can be had from the variables that are correlated with the population-size factor or factors (see Tables 49 and 50). The large urban centers of India are characterized among other things by relatively large areas, greater generalized accessibility (higher potentials),[2] greater accessibility to the railroad network, high ratio of telephone connections, and a high proportion of in-migrants, more particularly those in the age-groups 15-34 and 35-59 years. The characterization of large cities with greater accessibility is quite significant in the context of systems of cities, which, according to Berry, are "entities of interacting, interdependent parts,"[3] for it means that the larger cities play more central roles in these systems, in accordance with their size. This relationship may be seen in yet another way, for such cities serve as mediating agencies between populations involved in exchange relationships. Obviously, the mediating function of the city cannot be fulfilled without facilities for movement. "Transport routes and carriers must bring spatially separate populations within easy access of one another if exchange is to take place."[4] Once again, attention is drawn to the structure of the size factor, in other words, to the interrelationship of city size and various measures of accessibility and communication media. Thus, our empirical finding has a definite theoretical base.

Here, it would be interesting to recall some of the obser-

---

[1]Duncan, Metropolis and Region, p. 81.

[2]The term is borrowed from Duncan, *ibid*., p. 10.

[3]Berry, "Cities as Systems within Systems of Cities," p. 132.

[4]Schnore, *op. cit*., p. 409.

vations of Duncan about relationships of characteristics to size:

> 1. The larger the SMA, the more likely it is to have a diversified, i.e., less specialized, industrial structure.
> 2. . . . resource-extraction and first stage resource-using industries--are more highly developed in the less accessible SMA's, while second stage resource using industries and manufacturing industries making little direct use of resources are more conspicuous in the more accessible SMA'S.
> 3. The proportion of the labor force employed in manufacturing in hinterland SEA's (State Economic Areas) is found to increase with rising values of population potential (generalized accessibility) and also with increasing proximity to a metropolitan center.[1]

These observations seem to have validity in the context of Indian urbanization as well. The first generalization is true of all the major metropolitan centers of India with the possible exception of Ahmedabad.

The second generalization is only partly true of India or Indian cities. The major metropolitan centers in India, which also have greater accessibility, do not have the same high concentration of manufacturing activity in terms of the proportion of total labor force of the city, as witnessed in the more industrialized countries of the world. The present stage of industrial development in India reflects a dominant role of centralized planning and control so far as location of industries is concerned. Despite planned development, it seems that the present is just a transitional phase and in the long run the market will be the dominant factor in the location of industry in India.[2] Even now, such metropolitan centers as Ahmedabad, Bombay, Delhi, Calcutta, Bangalore, Madras, Kanpur, and Poona have considerable manufacturing activity. This leads us to Duncan's third generalization which, as he himself states, is in conformity with the observation of Harris that manufacturing is concentrated toward areas of high

---

[1] Duncan, Metropolis and Region, pp. 12, 15.

[2] This is a bold statement, as it ignores a number of other factors. In any event, an anticipation of future course of industrial growth in India is outside the scope of this study.

"market potential," and with the finding of Bogue that beyond a certain critical point intensity of manufacturing activity falls off as distance from the center of the metropolitan region increases. The validity of this generalization is reflected in the location of manufacturing centers in proximity to a major metropolitan center. In particular, note the location of cities in proximity to the metropolitan centers of Calcutta, Bombay, and Ahmedabad, most of which have considerable industrial activity.

Conversely, cities which have considerable proportion of workers in all categories of services (tertiary activity) are found either outside or on the margins of the zone of maximum generalized accessibility.

Last though not the least in importance is the first component, north-south regional differentiation by sex, the most fundamental characteristic of Indian urbanization. As noted before, this component accounts for the largest proportion of total variance of 102 Indian cities. According to the 1961 census, all cities except Eluru (Andhra Pradesh) had fewer women than men. The general paucity of women is again a characteristic of Indian or South Asian cities. However, cities in South India--Kerala, Madras, Mysore, and Andhra--have relatively larger number of females than cities in the north, particularly those of punjab, Uttar Pradesh, Madhya Pradesh, Bihar, West Bengal, and Assam. Cities in the states of Rajasthan, Gujarat, and Maharashtra occupy an intermediate position between the North and South extremes. Attempts have been made recently to give tentative reasons for the disparity in the female to male ratio in different regions of India.[1] However, the fact that cities with relatively more bal-

---

[1]See Lal, "Age and Sex Structure of Cities of India," and Sen, op. cit.

anced sex ratios are located in the four southern states which are also linguistic states with Malayalam, Tamil, Kanarese, and Telegu (all Dravidian languages) as the prevalent languages, it is argued, does not imply that the disparity in sex ratio is a reflection of the difference in the cultures of the two areas, namely north (the Aryan culture area) and south (the Dravidian culture area). Instead the emphasis is placed on such factors as male-selective migration to the manufacturing and administrative centers of northern and western India, as well as to destinations outside India, inmigration of relatively larger proportions of females from rural areas in the South, and the extremely small proportion of Muslims in the south.[1] The larger participation of women in the labor force of southern cities is ascribed to two other factors--higher literacy and greater proportion of Christian population in the south.[2]

Grouping Characteristics

Another major research finding is related to the grouping characteristics of Indian cities. For the first time, as a result of this study it has been possible to discern systematic spatial variations of the characteristics of Indian cities based on certain well-defined dimensions. Of particular interest is the north-south regional differentiation of cities by sex (female employment and sex ratio), literacy rate, and certain types of urban services. Equally interesting is the east-west regional differentiation of

---

[1]Note that Muslim population, in general, suffers from a highly unbalanced sex ratio (more males to females). There is a far greater proportion of Muslims in the north as compared with the south.

[2]More than 70 per cent of the total Christian population of India (10,726,350) is located in the four southern states of Andhra, Madras, Mysore, and Kerala. The last mentioned state has the largest proportion of Christian population of any states in India (21.22 per cent).

cities in terms of a number of characteristics, particularly migration. Cities in the western part of India have a relatively higher proportion of in-migrants from other urban centers, lower proportions of migrants from rural areas, lower proportions of workers, higher ratios of females to males, and higher proportions of female migrants than cities in the east. The western and eastern cities are also differentiated in terms of their distribution pattern. The Western cities are scattered while the eastern cities as in the extremely clustered nature of the Calcutta conurbation, are concentrated.

Yet another regional pattern embraces cities located in the Andhra-Madras littorals. These are characterized by large female employment, high sex ratios, very high proportions of female in-migrants and in-migrants from rural areas, large proportions of workers engaged in primary activity, low employment in manufacturing, relatively small population size, small area, and high density of dwellings per unit area.

Finally, the three grouping analyses of Indian cities have yielded a pattern which, interestingly enough, remains basically the same. As shown in the linkage trees, Indian cities fall into five *major* groups: (1) the national metropolises of Bombay, Delhi, and Calcutta; (2) Calcutta suburbs, a cluster of eight cities of more than 100,000 population; (3) Northern cities; (4) Southern cities; and (5) cities with generally central location, including most of the cities of Rajasthan, Madhya Pradesh and a few cities of Maharashtra and other states of India. The differences between these five major groups of Indian cities have already been mentioned in Chapter III. Their significance in terms of the dimensions of variation, particularly the first few components, is self-evident.

India's Urban System

This study of the properties of Indian cities permits a few observations concerning India's urban system. The introductory chapter showed that these cities form a system, since they clearly manifest a hierarchical arrangement (rank-size conformation). This study provides additional information about the interacting, interdependent parts of this system. Interdependence and interactance are measured through the use of potentials (measures of generalized accessibility) and distance to nearest metropolis (as indicator of metropolitan dominance). The association of hinterland economic activity with generalized accessibility reflects the interdependence of cities. Needless to say, this pattern of interdependence and interactance is strengthened by a relatively well-developed transport network, especially railroads on which these cities are prominent focal points.

As part of the urban system of India, the cities perform varied functions--as transport nodes (railroad junctions and ports), as centers of specialized function such as manufacturing, as central places with a heavy concentration of all types of services including administrative functions. In the latter case, some of the cities are "regional metropolises" and "regional capitals," while others like Bombay, Delhi and Calcutta are "national metropolises" occupying the uppermost level in some kind of hierarchical arrangement.

The advent of the British in India marked the beginning of political and social changes of great consequence, particularly to the economy of the country. Drastic changes in an economy must always leave their imprints on the urban scene. During this period which covers the last hundred years of the British rule, three factors, in particular, were responsible for the development of India's urban system. (1) The political integration of the entire sub-continent under a strong centralized system of government;[1] (2) the laying of an extensive railroad network, the sixth largest network in the world (fourth largest if Pakistan is included); (3) the establishment of factory industry, which, since 1947, has shown an increasingly rapid rate of growth.

As of today, it is not too difficult to visualize the entire population of India (439 million) being distributed in 538,439 villages, 2,552 towns, and 105 cities in a manner in which the cities occupy the uppermost level in some kind of hierarchy. In such a well-knit system cities play a dominant role in providing essential services to the lower-order centers, in the flow of goods from one point to the other, and as centers of specialized activity performing one service for large areas. In the words of Duncan, these metropolitan centers "occupy prominent focal points at which the patterns of interdependence are administered and mediated."[2]

Suggestions for Further Work in This Field

Several shortcomings and imperfections of the study are self-evident. Scarcity of desired data decreased the quality of the statistical analyses performed. What is needed is a more rigorous demonstration that India is beginning to have a metropolitan economy in which cities occupy "prominent focal points at which the patterns of interdependence are administered and mediated." For this we need a more representative set of variables such as per capita volume of wholesale and retail sales, business

---

[1]Although it applies, in reality, to the British India, the presence of the princely states did not retard the progress of urbanization. On the contrary, in many states, relatively minor towns gained in size and importance because of the concentration of political and commercial activity in these towns.

[2]Duncan, _Metropolis and Region_, p. 1.

service receipts, bank clearings, value added by manufacturing, household income, transport cost, a more refined set of housing and migration data and vital statistics, data on telephone calls, and measures of city-region linkage, to name a few.

Secondly, from the three grouping analyses which have yielded a strikingly similar pattern there is the very strong suggestion that there is some correlation between the regional pattern of cities and such aspects of Indian culture as language and to a lesser extent, religion, and with certain historical trends. The four major regional groups of cities, Southern cities, Northern cities, Central cities, and Calcutta suburbs, are correlated with the Dravidian language area,[1] the Hindi-speaking area, the extension of the Hindi-speaking area, and the Bengali-speaking area respectively. Likewise, Group VIII includes cities, which until 1947 and even in 1961, had considerable Muslim population. The growth pattern of cities in Groups IV, V, VII and XVI in particular and to some extent Group II, reflects certain historical trends of great consequences, such as the construction of the first railroads, the establishment of the first few mills and factories, and the opening of the first three major ports of India (Bombay, Calcutta, and Madras), in the Presidency provinces of Bombay, Bengal, and Madras.[2] To demonstrate such relationships, if indeed they exist, one needs data on the cultural attributes of cities.[3]

Finally, an effort has been made to demonstrate the usefulness of standardized statistical techniques in a study of Indian

---

[1]Marathi-speaking area being the exception.

[2]The Roman numerals refer to the original eighteen groups of political cities. See Table 26 and Fig. 6.

[3]As of today, the data on various languages spoken by cities and the religious composition cities are not available.

cities using a large number of variables. It was found that 72 per cent of the total variance of 102 cities could be explained by ten dimensions only. These ten dimensions were then utilized as a basis for classifying cities into subsets. The statistical groups which were established showed a marked regionalization. The statistical analysis, therefore, has high geographic quality. However, with the availability of more elaborate and refined set of data on Indian cities, it would be useful to repeat this analysis. Two principal points of emphasis remain: (1) the consistency of the components or dimensions of variation, and (2) the regional structure of Indian cities. The significance of the regional structure in terms of cultural attributes and historical trends should be properly assessed.

This study, in its present shape, provides insights into some of the major characteristics of Indian cities. It also underlines some of the major similarities and differences that exist between cities in Western and non-Western areas.

APPENDIX A

DEFINITION OF UNITS OF OBSERVATION

A political city as defined in this study consists of a municipal area together with a "railway colony," if there is any, but not a "railway settlement" which, as in the case of both Moradabad and Jhansi, is a "notified area."

A few notable exceptions to this definition are the following cities which in addition to "municipal areas" and "railway colonies" include other areas as indicated here:

Political City	Areas Other than "Railway Colonies" Included in the Political City
1. Delhi	New Delhi
2. Bangalore	Trust Board Area
3. Varanasi	Hindu University
4. Patna	Pataliputra Housing Colony
5. Meerut	Malyana
6. Kolhapur	Gandhinagar
7. Dehra Dun	Forest Research Institute and College Area
8. Thana	Kalwa

Furthermore, the political cities of Baroda, Rajkot, Bhavnagar and Jamnagar as defined in this study are the same as their respective town-groups.[1]

So far as Town-Groups are concerned the definition employed in this study remains the same as provided by the census except for Bombay and Calcutta. The town-group of Bombay also

[1]See A. Mitra, Census of India 1961, Vol. I, India, Part II-A(ii) (Delhi: Manager of Publications, 1963), p. 148.

includes Thana town group, and the town group of Calcutta consists of all the areas designated as urban within the "Calcutta Industrial Region."[1]

---

[1] *Ibid.*, pp. 168-81.

APPENDIX B

THE VARIABLES AND THEIR SOURCES[1]

Population Size and Structure

1. Enumerated population, census, 1961.
2. Total area of the city, 1961.
3. Population density, 1961.
4. Sex ratio: females per 1,000 males, 1961.
5. Sex ratio: females per 1,000 males, 1951.
6. Total literacy rate: literates per 1,000 population (aggregate).
7. Male literacy rate: male literates per 1,000 male population.
8. Persons belonging to Scheduled Castes per 1,000 aggregate population.

Population Change

9. Population change, 1941-1951--total change as per cent of 1941 population.
10. Population change, 1951-1961--total change as per cent of 1951 population.

Vital Statistics

11. Birth rate, 1960.
12. Death rate, 1960.
13. Infant death rate, 1960.
14. Maternal death rate, 1960

    Source: The Registrar General, India, Vital Statistics of India for 1960 (New Delhi: Ministry of Home Affairs, 1962).

---

[1]The principal source of data for a large number of variables remains the Census of India, 1961, unless indicated otherwise. The census volumes constantly referred to are: (1) Census of India 1961, Vol. I, India, Part II-A(i), (2) Census of India 1961, Vol. I, India, Part II-A(ii).

Housing and Households

15. Density of dwellings, 1961--"houses" (as defined in the census) per square mile of area of the city.

16. Average number of persons per 100 dwellings, 1961.

17. Average number of persons per 100 households, 1961.

Occupational Structure

18. Worker (or total labor force) as per cent of the total resident population, 1961.

19. Women as per cent of the total workers, 1961.

20. Per cent of cultivators, 1961.

21. Per cent of agricultural laborers, 1961.

22. Per cent of workers engaged in mining, quarrying, livestock, forestry, hunting, plantations and allied activities, 1961.

23. Per cent of workers engaged in household industry, 1961.

24. Per cent of workers engaged in manufacturing, 1961.

25. Per cent of workers engaged in construction, 1961.

26. Per cent of workers engaged in trade, 1961.

27. Per cent of workers engaged in transport, 1961.

28. Per cent of workers engaged in services, 1961.

29. Per cent of female cultivators, 1961.

30. Per cent of female agricultural laborers, 1961.

31. Per cent of women working in mining, quarrying, livestock, forestry, hunting, plantations, and allied activities, 1961.

32. Per cent of women working in household industry, 1961.

33. Per cent of women working in manufacturing, 1961.

34. Per cent of women working in construction, 1961.

35. Per cent of women working in trade, 1961.

36. Per cent of women working in transport, 1961.

37. Per cent of women working in service industry, 1961.

38. Per cent of workers engaged in primary industry (items 18, 19, and 20), 1961.

39. Per cent of workers engaged in secondary industry (items 21 and 22), 1961.

40. Per cent of workers engaged in tertiary industry (items 23 to 26), 1961.

Social Amenities (or Urban Services)

41. Telephone connections per 10,000 aggregate population, 1961.

42. Banks per 50,000 aggregate population, 1961.

Source: Items 41 and 42 are based on data contained in the telephone directories. See _The All India Telephone Directory_, Fourth edition, Parts I, II, and III (Baroda: The Indian Export Trade Journal, 1962).

Spatial Structure (Measures of Accessibility)

43. Distance to nearest city over 100,000 by road.

44. Distance to nearest city over 100,000 by railroad.

45. Distance to nearest city over a million by road.

46. Distance to nearest city over a million by railroad.

47. Total number of railroad routes radiating from a city.

Source: Items 43 and 45 are based on actual measurements of road distances on the map; in the case of items 44 and 46, railroad distances are obtained from a railway time-table. See _All India Railway Time-Table_ (Delhi: Railway Board, 1963); _Newman's Indian Bradshaw_ (Calcutta: W. Newman and Co., Ltd., 1964). For item 47 see _40 Mile Road Map of India_, Second edition (Delhi: Surveyor-General of India, 1956); _67-Mile Railway Map of India_, 1956 edition (Delhi: Surveyor-General of India, 1956).

48. Row co-ordinates.

49. Column co-ordinates.

Source: Items 48-49 are empirically derived.

50. Total population potentials, 1961.

51. Urban population potentials, 1961.

52. Literate population potentials, 1961.

53. Manufacturing population potentials, 1961.

Source: Items 50 to 53 were computed on the University of Chicago Computer System. The row and column coordinates were fed into the program to compute distances between cities. It may be noted that these four sets of potentials are measures of generalized accessibility <u>between cities</u>.

Migration

54. In-migrants as per cent of total population of a city, 1961.

55. Women as per cent of total in-migrants, 1961.

56. Per cent of in-migrants in the age group 0-14, 1961.

57. Per cent of in-migrants in the age group 15-34, 1961.

58. Per cent of in-migrants in the age group 35-59, 1961.

59. Per cent of in-migrants in the age group 60 or over, 1961.

60. Migrants originating from rural areas as per cent of total in-migrants, 1961.

61. Migrants originating from urban areas as per cent of total in-migrants, 1961.

62. Unclassified in-migrants as per cent of total in-migrants, 1961.

Source: For items 54 to 62 see Cenus of India, 1961.[1]

---

[1]The data on migration were made available by Professor N. R. Kar for class work. The author was one of the students who participated in his seminar on Indian urbanization offered at the University of Chicago in the Fall of 1964.

APPENDIX C

SUPPLEMENTARY TABLES

TABLE 48

INDIAN CITIES (POLITICAL)
CORRELATION MATRIX

Number	Name	1	2	3	4
1	TOTPOPLATION	1.000			
2	AREAINSQMILS	0.726	1.000		
3	POPLNDENSITY	0.216	-0.513	1.000	
4	POPCHGE51-61	-0.040	0.033	-0.094	1.000
5	POPCHGE41-51	0.109	0.228	-0.178	0.259
6	SEXRATIO1961	-0.134	-0.032	-0.138	-0.247
7	SEXRATIO1951	-0.223	-0.077	-0.185	-0.212
8	LITCYRATE'61	0.131	0.039	0.121	0.253
9	MALELITRAT61	0.101	0.077	0.025	0.214
10	DWELGPERSQML	0.189	-0.501	0.950	-0.028
11	PERS100DWLGS	-0.093	-0.064	-0.017	0.094
12	PERS100HSHLD	-0.075	-0.062	-0.006	0.011
13	BIRTHRATE'60	0.138	0.023	0.133	-0.100
14	DEATHRATE'60	0.174	0.005	0.206	-0.057
15	INFNTDRATE60	0.183	0.039	0.172	-0.003
16	MATNLDRATE60	-0.173	-0.053	-0.142	0.013
17	DISTCITYBYRD	0.013	0.171	-0.242	0.005
18	DISTCTYBYRRD	-0.013	0.231	-0.363	-0.063
19	DISTMCTYBYRD	0.405	0.412	-0.062	0.120
20	DISTMCITYRRD	0.278	0.340	-0.123	0.098
21	RAILRDROUTES	0.495	0.267	0.232	0.049
22	PRPSCHDCASTE	0.153	0.335	-0.295	-0.195
23	PCTOTWORKERS	0.046	-0.058	0.165	0.264
24	PCFEMWORKERS	-0.108	0.109	-0.293	-0.062
25	PCCULTVATORS	-0.258	0.094	-0.457	-0.225
26	PCAGRICLABOR	-0.348	-0.057	-0.350	-0.077
27	PCNTINMINING	-0.153	0.191	-0.463	-0.203
28	PCINHOUSHOLD	-0.060	-0.008	-0.080	-0.099
29	PCINMANUFCTG	0.213	-0.125	0.440	0.217
30	PCINCONSTRCT	0.113	0.356	-0.369	0.195
31	PRCNTINTRADE	0.157	-0.114	0.363	-0.139
32	PCINTRANSPRT	-0.028	0.060	-0.119	0.131
33	PCINSERVICES	-0.047	0.169	-0.293	0.058
34	PCFEMCULTVAT	0.013	0.292	-0.399	-0.053
35	PCFEMAGRLABR	-0.070	0.179	-0.342	-0.005

TABLE 48--Continued

5	6	7	8	9	10	11
1.000						
0.072	1.000					
0.044	0.926	1.000				
0.438	-0.173	-0.223	1.000			
0.464	0.020	-0.007	0.934	1.000		
-0.141	-0.186	-0.227	0.177	0.071	1.000	
-0.070	0.077	0.121	-0.110	-0.083	-0.199	1.000
0.012	0.175	0.212	0.151	0.190	-0.082	0.233
0.011	0.496	0.407	0.096	0.196	0.122	0.052
-0.033	0.278	0.210	0.009	0.096	0.141	0.218
-0.139	-0.196	-0.287	-0.019	-0.045	0.142	0.149
-0.178	0.012	0.094	-0.131	-0.090	-0.154	0.071
-0.084	0.275	0.365	-0.041	0.129	-0.257	0.102
-0.111	0.446	0.515	-0.098	0.099	-0.426	0.248
-0.016	-0.084	-0.064	0.171	0.216	-0.077	0.187
-0.035	0.034	0.062	0.198	0.250	-0.132	0.186
-0.110	-0.314	-0.347	-0.100	-0.166	0.240	-0.163
-0.126	0.001	0.009	-0.289	-0.211	-0.365	0.183
0.071	-0.470	-0.408	0.152	0.076	0.259	-0.055
0.189	0.722	0.711	0.016	0.245	-0.290	0.091
-0.004	0.375	0.416	-0.347	-0.228	-0.438	0.061
0.049	0.435	0.448	-0.144	-0.035	-0.284	0.038
0.124	0.380	0.369	-0.028	0.043	-0.467	0.046
-0.120	0.548	0.547	-0.397	-0.197	-0.128	0.254
0.187	-0.318	-0.390	0.232	0.119	0.474	-0.302
0.067	0.171	0.234	-0.076	0.025	-0.378	0.103
-0.181	0.083	0.030	-0.007	-0.027	0.282	0.157
-0.062	-0.099	0.011	0.082	0.097	-0.109	0.065
0.058	0.135	0.151	0.155	0.197	-0.348	0.303
0.257	0.347	0.348	-0.007	0.153	-0.387	-0.012
0.156	0.526	0.544	-0.012	0.178	-0.305	0.019

TABLE 48--Continued

Number	Name	1	2	3	4
36	PCTFEMMINING	0.066	0.125	-0.104	0.103
37	PCFEMHOUSHLD	-0.038	0.037	-0.089	0.004
38	PCFEMMANFCTG	-0.064	0.060	-0.164	-0.049
39	PCFEMCONSTRT	0.124	0.125	-0.029	0.046
40	PCNTFEMTRADE	0.021	0.178	-0.222	-0.090
41	PCFEMTRNSPRT	0.237	0.205	0.019	0.092
42	PCFEMSERVICE	-0.111	0.018	-0.168	-0.103
43	PCPRIMINDTRY	-0.320	0.099	-0.542	-0.166
44	PCSECINDSTRY	0.164	-0.169	0.438	0.175
45	PCTERTINDTRY	-0.017	0.157	-0.239	0.065
46	TELPER10000P	0.513	0.418	0.046	0.116
47	BANKPER50000	0.017	0.011	0.002	-0.010
48	POPPOTENTL61	0.447	0.189	0.309	0.087
49	ROWCOORDNATS	-0.046	-0.062	0.036	-0.112
50	COLCOORDNATS	-0.154	-0.191	0.093	0.068
51	URBANPOTENTL	0.522	0.211	0.383	-0.015
52	LITRATPOTNTL	0.521	0.338	0.189	-0.043
53	MFGPOTENTIAL	0.395	0.108	0.369	0.039
54	TOTALMIGRANT	0.758	0.559	0.186	0.035
55	FEMALMIGRANT	0.794	0.604	0.165	0.050
56	MIGRANTS0-14	0.776	0.588	0.166	0.076
57	MIGRANT15-34	0.742	0.546	0.185	0.035
58	MIGRANT35-59	0.757	0.549	0.200	0.012
59	MIGRANT60+YR	0.812	0.620	0.164	0.033
60	RURALMIGRANT	0.750	0.559	0.177	0.029
61	URBANMIGRANT	0.740	0.588	0.119	0.077
62	PROFMIGRANTS	0.070	0.081	-0.015	0.433
63	PRPFEMMIGRNT	-0.226	-0.039	-0.238	-0.264
64	PRPMGAGE0-14	-0.353	-0.192	-0.164	0.342
65	PRMGAGE15-34	0.244	0.090	0.181	0.109
66	PRMGAGE35-59	0.218	0.099	0.130	-0.392
67	PRMG60 YEARS	-0.035	0.112	-0.214	-0.323
68	PRPRURALMIGT	-0.056	-0.000	-0.063	-0.121
69	PRPURBANMIGT	0.090	0.117	-0.063	-0.036
70	PRUNCLASMIGT	-0.002	-0.078	0.108	0.150

TABLE 48--Continued

5	6	7	8	9	10	11
0.246	0.285	0.334	-0.038	0.124	-0.057	-0.068
0.236	0.353	0.336	0.232	0.312	-0.055	0.132
0.174	0.547	0.492	0.044	0.226	-0.142	-0.040
0.306	0.384	0.398	0.089	0.242	0.016	-0.055
0.161	0.455	0.467	-0.012	0.190	-0.210	0.061
0.374	0.118	0.067	0.387	0.438	0.063	-0.046
0.211	0.670	0.615	0.217	0.378	-0.139	-0.054
0.098	0.558	0.582	-0.233	-0.087	-0.519	0.105
0.110	-0.178	-0.259	0.069	0.014	0.458	-0.220
-0.037	0.085	0.162	0.094	0.140	-0.289	0.276
0.172	0.087	0.067	0.373	0.389	0.015	0.154
-0.002	0.429	0.433	0.296	0.380	-0.037	0.207
0.213	-0.546	-0.648	0.166	0.005	0.360	-0.304
0.282	0.503	0.475	0.370	0.457	0.051	-0.009
-0.109	-0.577	-0.507	0.042	-0.079	0.115	0.027
0.140	-0.494	-0.581	0.213	0.045	0.398	-0.243
-0.005	-0.366	-0.465	0.058	-0.091	0.167	-0.147
0.172	-0.532	-0.607	0.343	0.168	0.411	-0.297
0.181	-0.294	-0.376	0.226	0.153	0.198	-0.083
0.215	-0.247	-0.334	0.221	0.160	0.168	-0.070
0.218	-0.295	-0.379	0.226	0.151	0.176	-0.080
0.178	-0.293	-0.373	0.225	0.153	0.198	-0.083
0.161	-0.298	-0.382	0.226	0.154	0.212	-0.088
0.197	-0.246	-0.339	0.214	0.150	0.163	-0.062
0.179	-0.275	-0.357	0.218	0.156	0.192	-0.088
0.248	-0.221	-0.296	0.199	0.150	0.114	-0.044
0.283	-0.493	-0.535	0.397	0.273	0.100	-0.280
0.006	0.856	0.793	-0.319	-0.134	-0.299	0.178
0.103	-0.131	-0.089	0.029	0.008	-0.143	0.057
0.031	-0.261	-0.164	0.095	0.067	0.222	-0.042
-0.132	0.177	0.075	-0.033	-0.024	0.099	-0.091
-0.073	0.544	0.440	-0.209	-0.122	-0.283	0.166
-0.025	0.307	0.324	0.018	0.153	-0.036	0.045
0.157	0.222	0.261	-0.209	-0.142	-0.125	0.064
-0.079	-0.468	-0.512	0.121	-0.064	0.122	-0.090

TABLE 48--Continued

Number	Name	12	13	14	15
1	TOTPOPLATION				
2	AREAINSQMILS				
3	POPLNDENSITY				
4	POPCHGE51-61				
5	POPCHGE41-51				
6	SEXRATIO1961				
7	SEXRATIO1951				
8	LITCYRATE'61				
9	MALELITRAT61				
10	DWELGPERSQML				
11	PERSIOODWLGS				
12	PERSIOOHSHLD	1.000			
13	BIRTHRATE'60	0.043	1.000		
14	DEATHRATE'60	-0.076	0.676	1.000	
15	INFNTDRATE60	-0.259	0.115	0.463	1.000
16	MATNLDRATE60	-0.202	-0.137	0.129	0.186
17	DISTCITYBYRD	0.178	0.237	0.180	0.019
18	DISTCTYBYRRD	0.248	0.312	0.226	-0.033
19	DISTMCTYBYRD	0.027	0.042	0.099	0.098
20	DISTMCITYRRD	0.068	0.109	0.110	0.023
21	RAILRDROUTES	-0.232	-0.090	-0.033	0.044
22	PRPSCHDCASTE	-0.118	-0.010	0.046	0.188
23	PCTOTWORKERS	-0.361	-0.046	0.088	0.196
24	PCFEMWORKERS	0.171	0.418	0.296	-0.106
25	PCCULTVATORS	0.065	0.055	-0.102	-0.219
26	PCAGRICLABOR	-0.006	0.221	-0.029	-0.196
27	PCNTINMINING	0.152	0.107	0.033	-0.150
28	PCINHOUSHOLD	0.132	0.369	0.319	-0.024
29	PCINMANUFCTG	-0.163	-0.072	-0.016	0.098
30	PCINCONSTRCT	-0.108	-0.030	-0.069	-0.035
31	PRCNTINTRADE	-0.037	0.130	0.120	-0.012
32	PCINTRANSPRT	-0.092	-0.207	-0.125	-0.095
33	PCINSERVICES	0.338	0.088	0.017	-0.025
34	PCFEMCULTVAT	0.155	-0.028	-0.022	-0.073
35	PCFEMAGRLABR	0.063	0.193	0.103	-0.140

TABLE 48--Continued

16	17	18	19	20	21	22
1.000						
0.107	1.000					
0.130	0.813	1.000				
-0.070	0.132	0.234	1.000			
-0.066	0.173	0.297	0.914	1.000		
-0.108	-0.219	-0.223	0.138	-0.038	1.000	
0.101	0.175	0.316	0.051	-0.063	0.197	1.000
0.150	-0.100	-0.257	0.125	0.154	-0.011	-0.171
0.085	0.396	0.567	0.165	0.304	-0.452	-0.005
0.048	-0.011	0.225	-0.001	0.061	-0.187	0.194
0.035	-0.017	0.172	-0.102	-0.002	-0.250	-0.008
0.123	0.115	0.256	0.075	0.213	-0.370	0.100
0.061	0.376	0.480	0.128	0.193	-0.168	0.099
-0.136	-0.250	-0.463	-0.275	-0.333	0.206	-0.302
0.164	0.311	0.278	0.249	0.217	-0.005	0.124
-0.102	-0.254	-0.157	0.125	0.117	0.302	-0.081
0.078	0.145	0.113	0.196	0.227	0.147	-0.044
-0.029	0.195	0.385	0.346	0.379	-0.176	0.078
0.045	0.274	0.381	0.149	0.193	-0.243	0.101
0.106	0.379	0.446	0.192	0.258	-0.267	-0.072

TABLE 48--Continued

Number	Name	12	13	14	15
36	PCTFEMMINING	-0.011	0.132	0.113	-0.003
37	PCFEMHOUSHLD	0.168	0.227	0.247	-0.047
38	PCFEMMANFCTG	0.068	0.308	0.237	0.000
39	PCFEMCONSTRT	-0.141	0.243	0.229	0.023
40	PCNTFEMTRADE	-0.053	0.259	0.217	-0.011
41	PCFEMTRNSPRT	0.014	0.163	0.148	-0.069
42	PCFEMSERVICE	0.063	0.439	0.260	-0.121
43	PCPRIMINDTRY	0.133	0.171	-0.012	-0.250
44	PCSECINDSTRY	-0.159	0.017	0.085	0.065
45	PCTERTINDTRY	0.162	-0.038	-0.051	-0.085
46	TELPER10000P	0.231	0.299	0.226	-0.045
47	BANKPER50000	0.287	0.474	0.300	-0.041
48	POPPOTENTL61	-0.272	-0.276	-0.185	0.155
49	ROWCOORDNATS	0.099	0.471	0.279	-0.118
50	COLCOORDNATS	-0.175	-0.419	-0.228	0.016
51	URBANPOTENTL	-0.191	-0.165	-0.125	0.119
52	LITRATPOTNTL	-0.099	-0.099	-0.117	0.029
53	MFGPOTENTIAL	-0.118	-0.206	-0.174	0.065
54	TOTALMIGRANT	-0.072	0.028	0.038	0.130
55	FEMALMIGRANT	-0.076	0.057	0.061	0.127
56	MIGRANTS0-14	-0.080	0.021	0.025	0.138
57	MIGRANT15-34	-0.066	0.024	0.031	0.125
58	MIGRANT35-59	-0.074	0.030	0.048	0.134
59	MIGRANT60+YR	-0.078	0.077	0.092	0.133
60	RURALMIGRANT	-0.078	0.042	0.056	0.134
61	URBANMIGRANT	-0.065	0.057	0.057	0.111
62	PROPMIGRANTS	-0.381	-0.182	-0.180	0.070
63	PRPFEMMIGRNT	0.155	0.419	0.258	-0.180
64	PRPMGAGE0-14	0.016	-0.220	-0.187	0.034
65	PRMGAGE15-34	-0.013	-0.073	-0.079	-0.050
66	PRMGAGE35-59	-0.092	0.166	0.175	0.026
67	PRMG60 YEARS	0.157	0.425	0.320	-0.053
68	PRPRURALMIGT	0.001	0.287	0.250	0.034
69	PRPURBANMIGT	0.011	0.193	0.150	-0.015
70	PRUNCLASMIGT	-0.008	-0.428	-0.361	-0.026

TABLE 48--Continued

16	17	18	19	20	21	22
0.075	0.430	0.316	0.071	0.123	-0.107	-0.034
0.078	0.214	0.240	0.291	0.409	-0.413	-0.231
0.124	0.284	0.314	0.150	0.268	-0.424	-0.116
0.073	0.376	0.333	0.088	0.118	-0.249	0.020
0.090	0.301	0.380	0.248	0.344	-0.344	0.142
-0.051	0.054	0.036	0.192	0.199	-0.081	-0.167
0.029	0.285	0.350	0.029	0.197	-0.410	-0.077
0.112	0.084	0.340	0.004	0.142	-0.348	0.096
-0.119	-0.161	-0.352	-0.261	-0.297	0.172	-0.280
0.043	0.198	0.331	0.362	0.386	-0.003	0.080
-0.111	0.165	0.284	0.529	0.537	0.210	0.014
0.121	0.283	0.498	0.353	0.463	-0.212	-0.188
-0.183	-0.443	-0.708	-0.154	-0.290	0.405	-0.107
0.107	0.122	0.146	-0.046	0.102	-0.435	-0.253
0.018	-0.355	-0.441	-0.061	-0.027	0.141	0.059
-0.147	-0.445	-0.622	0.015	-0.087	0.348	-0.141
-0.257	-0.353	-0.337	0.202	0.149	0.434	-0.057
-0.141	-0.441	-0.645	-0.067	-0.146	0.260	-0.237
-0.140	-0.160	-0.214	0.455	0.312	0.306	-0.029
-0.148	-0.137	-0.173	0.453	0.300	0.343	0.008
-0.148	-0.153	-0.207	0.460	0.300	0.343	0.008
-0.137	-0.162	-0.215	0.446	0.305	0.293	-0.038
-0.138	-0.163	-0.221	0.461	0.324	0.294	-0.039
-0.148	-0.141	-0.170	0.469	0.326	0.365	0.017
-0.133	-0.143	-0.195	0.438	0.296	0.284	-0.036
-0.120	-0.114	-0.139	0.375	0.225	0.295	0.004
-0.055	-0.326	-0.380	-0.037	-0.084	0.233	-0.013
-0.053	0.181	0.400	-0.087	-0.012	-0.218	0.110
0.123	0.097	-0.055	-0.189	-0.236	-0.198	0.088
-0.135	-0.037	-0.032	0.186	0.137	0.198	-0.013
0.016	-0.147	-0.036	0.072	0.135	0.098	-0.128
-0.084	0.124	0.289	-0.036	0.066	-0.120	0.045
0.060	0.172	0.257	0.131	0.243	-0.275	-0.054
0.033	0.156	0.189	-0.033	-0.100	0.021	0.063
-0.084	-0.283	-0.394	-0.114	-0.186	0.273	0.014

TABLE 48--Continued

Number	Name	23	24	25	26
1	TOTPOPLATION				
2	AREAINSQMILS				
3	POPLNDENSITY				
4	POPCHGE51-61				
5	POPCHGE41-51				
6	SEXRATIO1961				
7	SEXRATIO1951				
8	LITCYRATE'61				
9	MALELITRAT61				
10	DWELGPERSQML				
11	PERSIOODWLGS				
12	PERSIOOHSHLD				
13	BIRTHRATE'60				
14	DEATHRATE'60				
15	INFNTDRATE60				
16	MATNLDRATE60				
17	DISTCITYBYRD				
18	DISTCTYBYRRD				
19	DISTMCTYBYRD				
20	DISTMCITYRRD				
21	RAILRDROUTES				
22	PRPSCHDCASTE				
23	PCTOTWORKERS	1.000			
24	PCFEMWORKERS	0.034	1.000		
25	PCCULTVATORS	-0.139	0.451	1.000	
26	PCAGRICLABOR	-0.021	0.510	0.699	1.000
27	PCNTINMINING	-0.189	0.384	0.357	0.237
28	PCINHOUSHOLD	-0.105	0.547	0.431	0.341
29	PCINMANUFCTG	0.283	-0.343	-0.503	-0.340
30	PCINCONSTRCT	-0.167	0.185	0.134	0.078
31	PRCNTINTRADE	-0.284	-0.263	-0.160	-0.107
32	PCINTRANSPRT	-0.127	-0.145	-0.245	-0.137
33	PCINSERVICES	-0.349	0.150	0.138	0.090
34	PCFEMCULTVAT	0.011	0.636	0.429	0.200
35	PCFEMAGRLABR	0.061	0.752	0.403	0.543

TABLE 48--Continued

27	28	29	30	31	32	33
1.000						
0.093	1.000					
-0.505	-0.310	1.000				
0.125	0.156	-0.235	1.000			
-0.182	0.022	-0.040	0.106	1.000		
-0.033	-0.170	-0.189	0.227	0.337	1.000	
0.221	0.050	-0.570	0.342	0.211	0.258	1.000
0.344	0.176	-0.233	0.182	-0.373	-0.105	0.072
0.226	0.432	-0.272	0.213	-0.261	-0.067	0.060

TABLE 48--Continued

Number	Name	23	24	25	26
36	PCTFEMMINING	0.159	0.532	0.161	0.169
37	PCFEMHOUSHLD	0.210	0.629	0.103	0.230
38	PCFEMMANFCTG	0.162	0.821	0.203	0.314
39	PCFEMCONSTRT	0.221	0.626	0.090	0.188
40	PCNTFEMTRADE	0.189	0.805	0.373	0.392
41	PCFEMTRNSPRT	0.254	0.383	-0.139	0.074
42	PCFEMSERVICE	0.090	0.834	0.226	0.366
43	PCPRIMINDTRY	-0.204	0.590	0.845	0.764
44	PCSECINDSTRY	0.341	-0.162	-0.360	-0.227
45	PCTERTINDTRY	-0.379	0.002	-0.023	-0.024
46	TELPER10000P	-0.126	0.101	-0.128	-0.141
47	BANKPER50000	-0.172	0.427	0.069	0.223
48	POPPOTENTL61	0.281	-0.553	-0.411	-0.362
49	ROWCOORDNATS	0.152	0.613	0.091	0.317
50	COLCOORDNATS	0.386	-0.430	-0.181	-0.155
51	URBANPOTENTL	0.327	-0.450	-0.397	-0.320
52	LITRATPOTNTL	0.054	-0.397	-0.205	-0.235
53	MFGPOTENTIAL	0.393	-0.429	-0.450	-0.323
54	TOTALMIGRANT	0.294	-0.122	-0.225	-0.258
55	FEMALMIGRANT	0.251	-0.102	-0.213	-0.252
56	MIGRANTS0-14	0.271	-0.140	-0.234	-0.269
57	MIGRANT15-34	0.298	-0.118	-0.220	-0.253
58	MIGRANT35-59	0.303	-0.121	-0.228	-0.258
59	MIGRANT60+YR	0.237	-0.115	-0.211	-0.258
60	RURALMIGRANT	0.312	-0.087	-0.209	-0.237
61	URBANMIGRANT	0.233	-0.081	-0.184	-0.233
62	PROPMIGRANTS	0.358	-0.293	-0.228	-0.117
63	PRPFEMMIGRNT	-0.447	0.615	0.469	0.488
64	PRPMGAGE0-14	0.048	-0.107	-0.119	-0.035
65	PRMGAGE15-34	0.167	-0.091	0.026	-0.085
66	PRMGAGE35-59	-0.054	0.080	-0.009	0.022
67	PRMG60 YEARS	-0.363	0.317	0.285	0.244
68	PRPRURALMIGT	0.300	0.592	0.251	0.370
69	PRPURBANMIGT	-0.256	0.098	0.143	0.046
70	PRUNCLASMIGT	-0.141	-0.682	-0.357	-0.416

TABLE 48--Continued

27	28	29	30	31	32	33
-0.051	0.295	0.020	0.245	-0.251	-0.018	-0.093
0.265	0.210	-0.094	0.066	-0.159	-0.069	0.056
0.243	0.347	-0.129	0.167	-0.202	-0.128	0.031
0.155	0.263	0.058	0.191	-0.244	-0.170	-0.195
0.317	0.381	-0.289	0.143	-0.305	-0.080	0.039
0.007	-0.023	0.196	-0.037	-0.134	-0.019	-0.025
0.400	0.284	-0.139	0.029	-0.226	-0.108	-0.034
0.682	0.413	-0.572	0.175	-0.145	-0.100	0.247
-0.533	0.072	0.881	-0.248	-0.097	-0.296	-0.661
0.127	-0.043	-0.553	0.449	0.461	0.687	0.836
0.146	0.079	-0.179	0.236	0.440	0.282	0.533
0.209	0.326	-0.253	0.150	0.288	0.172	0.450
-0.378	-0.519	0.547	-0.190	-0.004	-0.173	-0.377
0.307	0.143	-0.023	-0.132	-0.215	-0.175	-0.071
-0.171	-0.339	0.047	-0.210	-0.073	0.161	-0.111
-0.304	-0.515	0.449	-0.185	0.137	-0.120	-0.288
-0.173	-0.306	0.266	-0.017	0.275	-0.074	-0.049
-0.302	-0.580	0.524	-0.290	0.028	-0.127	-0.351
-0.110	-0.222	0.181	0.031	0.150	0.008	-0.026
-0.103	-0.198	0.179	0.055	0.148	-0.003	-0.014
-0.131	-0.233	0.184	0.046	0.140	0.007	-0.010
-0.102	-0.221	0.176	0.028	0.147	0.010	-0.024
-0.112	-0.223	0.186	0.022	0.156	0.007	-0.039
-0.104	-0.185	0.171	0.060	0.179	-0.011	-0.011
-0.102	-0.201	0.183	0.010	0.121	0.001	-0.044
-0.058	-0.170	0.171	0.066	0.102	-0.006	-0.017
-0.166	-0.522	0.327	0.035	-0.015	0.123	-0.142
0.308	0.503	-0.374	0.151	0.142	-0.032	0.153
-0.185	-0.135	-0.068	0.048	-0.140	0.217	0.085
-0.038	-0.067	0.041	0.071	-0.010	0.028	0.079
0.142	0.051	0.160	-0.168	0.103	-0.229	-0.234
0.288	0.405	-0.235	0.077	0.205	-0.158	0.074
0.154	0.315	-0.161	-0.191	-0.264	-0.126	-0.022
0.078	0.173	-0.023	0.237	0.017	-0.008	0.045
-0.212	-0.443	0.182	0.040	0.264	0.137	-0.007

TABLE 48--Continued

Number	Name	34	35	36	37
1	TOTPOPLATION				
2	AREAINSQMILS				
3	POPLNDENSITY				
4	POPCHGE51-61				
5	POPCHGE41-51				
6	SEXRATIO1961				
7	SEXRATIO1951				
8	LITCYRATE'61				
9	MALELITRAT61				
10	DWELGPERSQML				
11	PERS100DWLGS				
12	PERS100HSHLD				
13	BIRTHRATE'60				
14	DEATHRATE'60				
15	INFNTDRATE60				
16	MATNLDRATE60				
17	DISTCITYBYRD				
18	DISTCTYBYRRD				
19	DISTMCTYBYRD				
20	DISTMCITYRRD				
21	RAILRDROUTES				
22	PRPSCHDCASTE				
23	PCTOTWORKERS				
24	PCFEMWORKERS				
25	PCCULTVATORS				
26	PCAGRICLABOR				
27	PCNTINMINING				
28	PCINHOUSHOLD				
29	PCINMANUFCTG				
30	PCINCONSTRCT				
31	PRCNTINTRADE				
32	PCINTRANSPRT				
33	PCINSERVICES				
34	PCFEMCULTVAT	1.000			
35	PCFEMAGRLABR	0.643	1.000		

TABLE 48--Continued

38	39	40	41	42	43	44

TABLE 48--Continued

Number	Name	34	35	36	37
36	PCTFEMMINING	0.511	0.559	1.000	
37	PCFEMHOUSHLD	0.337	0.457	0.354	1.000
38	PCFEMMANFCTG	0.531	0.645	0.508	0.651
39	PCFEMCONSTRT	0.511	0.532	0.570	0.417
40	PCNTFEMTRADE	0.541	0.606	0.469	0.490
41	PCFEMTRNSPRT	0.289	0.338	0.175	0.406
42	PCFEMSERVICE	0.528	0.619	0.402	0.566
43	PCPRIMINDTRY	0.435	0.491	0.121	0.247
44	PCSECINDSTRY	-0.188	-0.135	0.104	-0.042
45	PCTERTINDTRY	-0.031	-0.011	-0.090	-0.026
46	TELPER10000P	0.029	0.047	0.016	0.144
47	BANKPER50000	0.064	0.328	0.135	0.425
48	POPPOTENTL61	-0.233	-0.362	-0.156	-0.306
49	ROWCOORDNATS	0.242	0.437	0.200	0.501
50	COLCOORDNATS	-0.403	-0.462	-0.399	-0.275
51	URBANPOTENTL	-0.218	-0.330	-0.240	-0.139
52	LITRATPOTNTL	-0.224	-0.299	-0.304	-0.104
53	MFGPOTENTIAL	-0.201	-0.320	-0.257	-0.108
54	TOTALMIGRANT	0.078	-0.048	-0.024	0.054
55	FEMALMIGRANT	0.097	-0.029	0.006	0.034
56	MIGRANTS0-14	0.076	-0.051	-0.005	0.021
57	MIGRANT15-34	0.084	-0.043	-0.023	0.053
58	MIGRANT35-59	0.068	-0.053	-0.036	0.075
59	MIGRANT60+YR	0.076	-0.050	-0.012	0.045
60	RURALMIGRANT	0.102	-0.015	0.002	0.054
61	URBANMIGRANT	0.145	0.008	0.031	-0.010
62	PROPMIGRANTS	-0.098	-0.213	-0.082	-0.124
63	PRPFEMMIGRNT	0.287	0.419	0.208	0.263
64	PRPMGAGE0-14	-0.105	-0.016	0.016	-0.130
65	PRMGAGE15-34	0.037	-0.099	0.065	-0.118
66	PRMGAGE35-59	0.035	0.027	-0.105	0.205
67	PRMG60 YEARS	0.115	0.190	0.037	0.176
68	PRPRURALMIGT	0.271	0.400	0.232	0.333
69	PRPURBANMIGT	0.210	0.240	0.222	-0.080
70	PRUNCLASMIGT	-0.422	-0.576	-0.391	-0.293

TABLE 48--Continued

38	39	40	41	42	43	44
1.000						
0.585	1.000					
0.667	0.602	1.000				
0.444	0.517	0.453	1.000			
0.701	0.608	0.711	0.459	1.000		
0.328	0.170	0.437	-0.040	0.414	1.000	
-0.020	0.131	-0.131	0.159	-0.041	-0.473	1.000
-0.067	-0.216	-0.053	-0.070	-0.124	0.115	-0.685
-0.002	0.036	0.025	0.205	0.062	0.014	-0.265
0.266	0.101	0.195	0.119	0.358	0.266	-0.234
-0.289	-0.142	-0.272	0.138	-0.373	-0.560	0.427
0.556	0.414	0.594	0.438	0.745	0.294	0.041
-0.329	-0.346	-0.149	-0.074	-0.297	-0.275	0.048
-0.191	-0.122	-0.194	0.226	-0.296	0.500	0.315
-0.247	-0.256	-0.304	0.080	-0.368	-0.294	0.145
-0.164	-0.120	-0.181	0.288	-0.214	-0.529	0.386
-0.018	0.054	0.020	0.301	-0.117	-0.261	0.094
-0.023	0.070	0.017	0.296	-0.106	-0.245	0.093
-0.035	0.050	0.001	0.285	-0.138	-0.275	0.091
-0.019	0.052	0.020	0.294	-0.114	-0.253	0.090
-0.005	0.059	0.034	0.319	-0.110	-0.267	0.101
-0.025	0.054	-0.002	0.296	-0.122	-0.247	0.092
0.004	0.076	0.062	0.311	-0.080	-0.242	0.107
-0.039	0.073	0.016	0.257	-0.095	-0.194	0.092
-0.159	0.017	-0.237	0.152	-0.195	-0.246	0.124
0.418	0.230	0.352	0.013	0.524	0.579	-0.220
0.033	-0.077	-0.045	-0.067	-0.088	-0.132	-0.085
-0.277	0.060	-0.035	-0.031	-0.201	-0.044	-0.024
0.116	0.049	0.089	0.158	0.199	0.039	0.190
0.246	0.004	0.015	-0.075	0.253	0.371	-0.113
0.477	0.302	0.659	0.239	0.582	0.305	0.016
0.013	0.186	0.082	0.064	-0.005	0.144	-0.051
-0.505	-0.439	-0.741	-0.291	-0.602	-0.414	0.018

TABLE 48--Continued

Number	Name	45	46	47	48	49
36	PCTFEMMINING					
37	PCFEMHOUSHLD					
38	PCFEMMANFCTG					
39	PCFEMCONSTRT					
40	PCNTFEMTRADE					
41	PCFEMTRNSPRT					
42	PCFEMSERVICE					
43	PCPRIMINDTRY					
44	PCSECINDSTRY					
45	PCTERTINDTRY	1.000				
46	TELPER10000P	0.551	1.000			
47	BANKPER50000	0.413	0.601	1.000		
48	POPPOTENTL61	-0.364	-0.160	-0.618	1.000	
49	ROWCOORDNATS	-0.194	0.055	0.395	-0.160	1.000
50	COLCOORDNATS	-0.043	-0.275	-0.459	0.347	-0.164
51	URBANPOTENTL	-0.248	0.012	-0.398	0.884	-0.061
52	LITRATPOTNTL	-0.024	0.255	-0.156	0.534	-0.318
53	MFGPOTENTIAL	-0.328	-0.067	-0.394	0.869	0.058
54	TOTALMIGRANT	0.006	0.392	-0.025	0.510	-0.033
55	FEMALMIGRANT	0.010	0.414	-0.007	0.500	-0.028
56	MIGRANTS0-14	0.016	0.395	-0.034	0.527	-0.052
57	MIGRANT15-34	0.007	0.385	-0.024	0.502	-0.031
58	MIGRANT35-59	-0.004	0.389	-0.025	0.510	-0.023
59	MIGRANT60+YR	0.016	0.441	0.003	0.497	-0.050
60	RURALMIGRANT	-0.020	0.374	-0.021	0.493	0.007
61	URBANMIGRANT	0.000	0.375	-0.007	0.468	-0.001
62	PROPMIGRANTS	-0.051	0.047	-0.243	0.391	-0.264
63	PRPFEMMIGRNT	0.130	-0.031	0.304	-0.559	0.283
64	PRPMGAGE0-14	0.139	-0.285	-0.173	0.025	-0.067
65	PRMGAGE15-34	0.081	0.263	-0.023	0.080	-0.205
66	PRMGAGE35-59	-0.272	0.040	0.121	0.064	0.259
67	PRMG60 YEARS	0.021	0.117	0.263	-0.380	0.081
68	PRPRURALMIGT	-0.163	-0.032	0.240	-0.251	0.577
69	PRPURBANMIGT	0.068	0.095	0.117	-0.089	0.062
70	PRUNCLASMIGT	0.124	-0.030	-0.329	0.321	-0.642

TABLE 48--Continued

50	51	52	53	54	55	56	57
1.000							
0.280	1.000						
0.035	0.730	1.000					
0.353	0.954	0.617	1.000				
-0.064	0.707	0.584	0.615	1.000			
-0.103	0.674	0.559	0.573	0.991	1.000		
-0.061	0.695	0.565	0.598	0.990	0.995	1.000	
-0.067	0.701	0.575	0.612	0.999	0.988	0.987	1.000
-0.054	0.718	0.600	0.629	0.997	0.981	0.980	0.996
-0.101	0.683	0.604	0.569	0.983	0.992	0.985	0.978
-0.071	0.677	0.536	0.599	0.993	0.985	0.982	0.993
-0.146	0.618	0.486	0.530	0.961	0.978	0.966	0.963
0.246	0.353	0.261	0.364	0.257	0.250	0.281	0.256
-0.450	-0.511	-0.318	-0.563	-0.307	-0.264	-0.306	-0.306
0.256	-0.105	-0.332	-0.044	-0.241	-0.246	-0.178	-0.244
-0.035	0.120	0.140	0.054	0.263	0.261	0.240	0.276
-0.105	0.158	0.263	0.177	0.121	0.117	0.071	0.114
-0.414	-0.298	0.045	-0.372	-0.148	-0.122	-0.167	-0.152
0.067	-0.198	-0.338	-0.112	-0.032	-0.031	-0.044	-0.032
-0.448	-0.088	0.014	-0.170	-0.020	0.017	-0.002	-0.019
0.230	0.266	0.343	0.230	0.047	0.021	0.056	0.047

TABLE 48--Continued

Number	Name	58	59	60	61	62
36	PCTFEMMINING					
37	PCFEMHOUSHLD					
38	PCFEMMANFCTG					
39	PCFEMCONSTRT					
40	PCNTFEMTRADE					
41	PCFEMTRNSPRT					
42	PCFEMSERVICE					
43	PCPRIMINDTRY					
44	PCSECINDSTRY					
45	PCTERTINDTRY					
46	TELPER10000P					
47	BANKPER50000					
48	POPPOTENTL61					
49	ROWCOORDNATS					
50	COLCOORDNATS					
51	URBANPOTENTL					
52	LITRATPOTNTL					
53	MFGPOTENTIAL					
54	TOTALMIGRANT					
55	FEMALMIGRANT					
56	MIGRANTS0-14					
57	MIGRANT15-34					
58	MIGRANT35-59	1.000				
59	MIGRANT60+YR	0.976	1.000			
60	RURALMIGRANT	0.990	0.968	1.000		
61	URBANMIGRANT	0.943	0.957	0.963	1.000	
62	PROPMIGRANTS	0.245	0.244	0.235	0.232	1.000
63	PRPFEMMIGRNT	-0.312	-0.262	-0.292	-0.240	-0.477
64	PRPMGAGE0-14	-0.262	-0.277	-0.242	-0.217	0.180
65	PRMGAGE15-34	0.252	0.244	0.252	0.257	0.252
66	PRMGAGE35-59	0.156	0.144	0.136	0.085	-0.309
67	PRMG60 YEARS	-0.143	-0.054	-0.156	-0.123	-0.359
68	PRPRURALMIGT	-0.024	-0.052	0.040	-0.045	-0.327
69	PRPURBANMIGT	-0.033	0.007	-0.031	0.114	-0.154
70	PRUNCLASMIGT	0.047	0.050	-0.021	-0.030	0.443

TABLE 48--Continued

63	64	65	66	67	68	69	70
1.000							
-0.066	1.000						
-0.327	-0.419	1.000					
0.131	-0.699	-0.283	1.000				
0.602	-0.374	-0.337	0.371	1.000			
0.245	-0.126	-0.130	0.254	0.083	1.000		
0.207	0.048	0.014	-0.101	0.048	-0.381	1.000	
-0.393	0.099	0.125	-0.197	-0.118	-0.785	-0.273	1.000

TABLE 49

INDIAN CITIES (POLITICAL)
MATRIX OF FACTOR LOADINGS

Variable					
Number	Name	Communality	1	2	3
1	TOTPOPLATION	0.835	0.052	0.436	0.093
2	AREAINSQMILS	0.866	0.143	0.317	0.170
3	POPLNDENSITY	0.838	-0.135	0.116	-0.115
4	POPCHGE51-61	0.483	-0.007	0.000	0.068
5	POPCHGE41-51	0.614	0.233	0.280	-0.097
6	SEXRATIO1961	0.897	0.492	-0.324	0.091
7	SEXRATIO1951	0.861	0.500	-0.439	0.139
8	LITCYRATE'61	0.868	0.099	0.163	0.112
9	MALELITRAT61	0.800	0.288	0.039	0.145
10	DWELGPERSQML	0.845	-0.084	0.186	-0.152
11	PERSIOODWLGS	0.297	-0.061	-0.379	0.233
12	PERSIOOHSHLD	0.625	-0.068	-0.492	-0.016
13	BIRTHRATE'60	0.757	0.272	-0.174	-0.021
14	DEATHRATE'60	0.789	0.222	-0.145	-0.013
15	INFNTDRATE60	0.583	-0.056	0.048	-0.069
16	MATNLDRATE60	0.280	0.143	-0.080	0.107
17	DISTCITYBYRD	0.741	0.357	-0.574	0.078
18	DISTCTYBYRRD	0.821	0.348	-0.664	0.194
19	DISTMCTYBYRD	0.761	0.242	-0.012	0.529
20	DISTMCITYRRD	0.806	0.348	-0.089	0.554

TABLE 49--Continued

Normal Varimax Rotated Factor Loadings						
4	5	6	7	8	9	10
0.121	0.402	0.135	-0.013	0.202	0.592	0.217
0.681	0.164	0.062	-0.019	0.204	0.417	0.077
-0.817	0.262	0.075	0.001	-0.060	0.151	0.159
-0.039	0.097	-0.651	-0.204	0.040	0.003	0.003
0.165	-0.092	-0.270	-0.532	0.269	-0.031	-0.083
-0.050	-0.305	0.434	-0.037	0.474	-0.178	0.022
-0.045	-0.303	0.315	0.040	0.413	-0.170	-0.064
-0.106	0.156	-0.207	-0.847	-0.141	0.063	0.014
-0.051	0.128	-0.182	-0.798	-0.046	0.057	0.032
-0.833	0.210	-0.030	-0.019	-0.088	0.153	0.102
0.070	-0.026	0.036	0.022	-0.103	0.021	0.277
0.027	0.096	0.249	-0.417	0.013	0.134	-0.339
-0.200	-0.161	0.259	-0.256	0.308	0.108	0.589
-0.148	0.046	0.168	-0.081	0.140	0.055	0.798
0.069	0.232	-0.092	0.119	-0.123	-0.008	0.690
0.130	0.024	-0.109	0.234	-0.135	-0.297	0.227
0.260	0.401	-0.062	0.043	0.202	0.036	0.053
0.345	0.129	0.083	0.021	0.210	0.140	0.119
0.130	0.143	-0.037	0.001	-0.210	0.577	0.078
0.095	0.044	0.035	-0.065	-0.281	0.523	0.035

TABLE 49--Continued

Variable					
Number	Name	Communality	1	2	3
21	RAILRDROUTES	0.576	-0.336	0.408	0.109
22	PRPSCHDCASTE	0.547	-0.142	-0.091	-0.011
23	PCTOTWORKERS	0.775	0.321	0.293	-0.217
24	PCFEMWORKERS	0.931	0.843	-0.309	0.023
25	PCCULTVATORS	0.835	0.209	-0.205	-0.087
26	PCAGRICLABOR	0.721	0.352	-0.095	-0.013
27	PCNTINMINING	0.585	0.188	-0.165	0.079
28	PCINHOUSHOLD	0.666	0.365	-0.498	-0.026
29	PCINMANUFCTG	0.777	-0.064	0.409	-0.473
30	PCINCONSTRCT	0.539	0.141	-0.025	0.447
31	PRCNTINTRADE	0.806	-0.310	0.156	0.591
32	PCINTRANSPRT	0.650	-0.064	-0.007	0.723
33	PCINSERVICES	0.720	-0.116	-0.344	0.635
34	PCFEMCULTVAT	0.665	0.597	-0.105	-0.105
35	PCFEMAGRLABR	0.728	0.758	-0.167	0.042
36	PCTFEMMINING	0.672	0.627	-0.158	-0.092
37	PCFEMHOUSHLD	0.550	0.650	-0.105	0.099
38	PCFEMMANFCTG	0.739	0.831	-0.053	0.045
39	PCFEMCONSTRT	0.695	0.744	0.002	-0.156
40	PCNTFEMTRADE	0.800	0.843	-0.064	0.031
41	PCFEMTRNSPRT	0.583	0.576	0.327	0.042

TABLE 49--Continued

Normal Varimax Rotated Factor Loadings						
4	5	6	7	8	9	10
-0.089	0.165	-0.037	0.298	0.182	0.345	0.089
0.567	0.020	-0.002	0.295	0.072	0.022	0.323
-0.163	0.052	-0.441	0.080	-0.498	0.129	0.209
0.119	-0.262	0.100	-0.098	0.136	0.025	0.046
0.298	-0.742	0.076	0.243	0.070	0.125	-0.133
0.041	-0.755	0.018	0.073	0.055	-0.077	-0.040
0.466	-0.412	0.273	-0.225	-0.055	-0.003	-0.037
-0.081	-0.182	0.164	0.323	0.233	0.173	0.171
-0.414	0.396	-0.140	-0.134	0.128	-0.003	-0.018
0.302	0.012	-0.223	0.156	0.385	0.042	-0.050
-0.439	-0.066	0.248	0.046	0.239	0.055	0.128
-0.034	0.168	-0.191	0.076	-0.006	-0.177	-0.143
0.268	-0.136	-0.011	-0.286	0.007	0.112	0.017
0.418	-0.080	-0.041	-0.024	0.165	0.144	-0.234
0.147	-0.189	-0.038	0.041	0.214	0.047	-0.124
0.009	0.132	-0.281	0.146	0.332	0.099	-0.088
-0.043	-0.027	0.116	-0.278	-0.095	0.061	-0.017
0.039	-0.040	0.104	-0.070	0.068	-0.139	0.012
0.023	0.062	-0.178	-0.025	0.264	0.058	0.087
0.178	-0.166	0.010	0.061	-0.097	0.042	0.103
-0.020	0.139	-0.033	-0.343	0.018	0.053	0.016

TABLE 49--Continued

Variable					
Number	Name	Communality	1	2	3
42	PCFEMSERVICE	0.824	0.807	-0.116	-0.039
43	PCPRIMINDTRY	0.920	0.309	-0.265	0.052
44	PCSECINDSTRY	0.751	0.082	0.263	-0.564
45	PCTERTINDTRY	0.923	-0.159	-0.222	0.894
46	TELPER10000P	0.841	0.023	-0.033	0.572
47	BANKPER50000	0.754	0.280	-0.415	0.456
48	POPPOTENTL61	0.866	-0.234	0.791	-0.279
49	ROWCOORDNATS	0.799	0.675	-0.012	-0.099
50	COLCOORDNATS	0.724	-0.272	0.259	0.030
51	URBANPOTENTL	0.844	-0.154	0.823	-0.102
52	LITRATPOTNTL	0.731	-0.297	0.621	0.087
53	MFGPOTENTIAL	0.881	-0.105	0.781	-0.192
54	PROPMIGRANTS	0.741	-0.191	0.502	-0.001
55	PRPFEMMIGRNT	0.814	0.341	-0.304	0.124
56	PRPMGAGE0-14	0.728	-0.056	-0.088	0.119
57	PRMGAGE15-34	0.696	-0.142	-0.039	-0.046
58	PRMGAGE35-59	0.692	0.186	0.242	-0.117
59	PRMG60 YEARS	0.630	0.061	-0.192	0.018
60	PRPRURALMIGT	0.748	0.653	-0.159	-0.083
61	PRPURBANMIGT	0.445	0.059	-0.035	-0.001
62	PRUNCLASMIGT	0.678	-0.719	0.188	0.088

TABLE 49--Continued

Normal Varimax Rotated Factor Loadings						
4	5	6	7	8	9	10
0.013	-0.173	0.183	-0.261	0.061	-0.140	0.055
0.328	-0.776	0.152	0.024	0.093	0.015	-0.092
-0.467	0.345	-0.076	0.047	0.104	0.026	0.032
0.154	-0.023	-0.065	-0.101	0.085	-0.001	-0.053
0.009	0.084	0.047	-0.385	0.196	0.532	0.184
-0.197	-0.101	0.170	-0.360	0.127	0.194	0.187
-0.051	0.291	-0.105	-0.025	-0.076	0.044	-0.035
-0.137	-0.149	0.230	-0.425	-0.089	-0.178	0.138
-0.026	0.016	-0.186	0.127	-0.697	-0.212	-0.017
-0.109	0.250	0.041	-0.087	-0.141	0.170	-0.006
0.011	0.125	0.216	-0.023	0.045	0.428	-0.044
-0.146	0.285	0.017	-0.211	-0.258	0.066	-0.079
0.026	-0.073	-0.620	-0.243	-0.009	0.008	0.053
0.023	-0.389	0.431	0.103	0.433	-0.230	0.040
0.110	0.143	-0.470	0.001	-0.041	-0.668	-0.039
-0.122	-0.136	-0.420	-0.017	0.011	0.675	-0.081
-0.082	0.046	0.726	0.023	-0.111	0.180	0.066
0.114	-0.222	0.626	-0.020	0.332	0.012	0.157
-0.046	-0.156	0.189	0.026	-0.441	0.026	0.176
0.095	-0.022	-0.064	0.093	0.642	0.017	0.069
-0.016	0.177	-0.154	-0.089	0.029	-0.038	-0.230

TABLE 50

INDIAN TOWN GROUPS
MATRIX OF FACTOR LOADINGS

Variable			Normal Varimax Rotated Factor Loadings		
Number	Name	Communality	1	2	3
1	TOTPOPLATION	0.883	-0.083	0.874	0.168
2	AREAINSQMILS	0.911	-0.104	0.751	-0.438
3	POPLNDENSITY	0.883	0.047	0.053	0.856
4	POPCHGE51-61	0.708	-0.170	-0.151	-0.081
5	POPCHGE41-51	0.562	0.145	0.211	-0.050
6	SEXRATIO1961	0.903	0.738	-0.118	0.067
7	SEXRATIO1951	0.820	0.743	-0.279	-0.001
8	LITCYRATE'61	0.858	0.094	0.050	0.092
9	MALELITRAT61	0.784	0.259	0.002	0.018
10	DWELGPERSQML	0.825	0.079	0.035	0.824
11	PERSIOODWLGS	0.427	-0.085	-0.300	0.130
12	PERSIOOHSHLD	0.656	-0.060	-0.085	-0.023
13	BIRTHRATE'60	0.700	0.265	0.044	0.088
14	DEATHRATE'60	0.790	0.152	0.001	0.186
15	INFNTDRATE60	0.625	-0.205	0.003	0.179
16	MATNLDRATE60	0.430	0.110	-0.171	-0.114
17	DISTCITYBYRD	0.766	0.217	-0.010	0.078
18	DISTCTYBYRRD	0.816	0.116	-0.143	-0.040

TABLE 50--Continued

Normal Varimax Rotated Factor Loadings						
4	5	6	7	8	9	10
-0.041	0.118	-0.165	0.166	0.021	-0.011	0.115
0.032	0.099	-0.239	0.214	-0.172	-0.015	-0.022
-0.095	0.009	0.107	-0.112	0.283	-0.005	0.180
-0.360	0.388	-0.445	0.080	-0.402	0.059	-0.006
-0.055	0.673	0.155	-0.109	-0.016	-0.016	0.042
0.146	-0.247	0.349	-0.075	0.165	0.270	0.177
0.001	-0.237	0.254	-0.091	-0.088	0.206	0.102
0.168	0.803	-0.258	0.105	0.158	0.218	0.126
0.103	0.755	-0.249	0.155	0.107	0.175	0.087
0.182	0.090	0.055	-0.168	0.225	0.004	0.126
0.254	-0.026	-0.202	0.160	0.218	-0.295	0.217
0.076	0.041	0.185	0.402	0.594	0.276	-0.110
-0.044	0.096	0.027	-0.062	0.139	0.203	0.738
-0.131	0.048	0.009	-0.006	-0.161	-0.010	0.828
0.061	0.077	-0.038	0.242	-0.323	-0.259	0.557
0.044	-0.014	0.132	0.037	-0.565	0.040	0.185
0.026	-0.019	0.008	0.840	-0.075	-0.026	0.004
0.117	0.048	-0.172	0.852	0.015	-0.063	0.070

TABLE 50--Continued

Variable			Normal Varimax Rotated Factor Loadings		
Number	Name	Communality	1	2	3
19	DISTMCTYBYRD	0.834	-0.012	0.187	0.036
20	DISTMCITYRRD	0.882	0.106	0.053	-0.048
21	RAILRDROUTES	0.598	-0.389	0.562	0.237
22	PRPSCHDCASTE	0.677	-0.180	0.056	-0.260
23	PCTOTWORKERS	0.775	0.122	-0.049	-0.155
24	PCFEMWORKERS	0.931	0.883	-0.214	-0.218
25	PCCULTVATORS	0.780	0.263	-0.178	-0.662
26	PCAGRICLABOR	0.609	0.475	-0.185	-0.411
27	PCNTINMINING	0.511	0.166	-0.079	-0.647
28	PCINHOUSHOLD	0.667	0.365	-0.251	0.004
29	PCINMANUFCTG	0.789	-0.066	0.290	0.424
30	PCINCONSTRCT	0.652	-0.001	0.092	-0.149
31	PRCNTINTRADE	0.756	-0.163	0.146	0.577
32	PCINTRANSPRT	0.636	-0.152	-0.049	0.318
33	PCINSERVICES	0.736	-0.254	-0.157	-0.114
34	PCFEMCULTVAT	0.535	0.384	0.097	-0.419
35	PCFEMAGRLABR	0.685	0.703	-0.069	-0.256
36	PCTFEMMINING	0.549	0.520	-0.035	0.101

TABLE 50--Continued

Normal Varimax Rotated Factor Loadings						
4	5	6	7	8	9	10
0.118	0.043	-0.875	0.109	-0.021	-0.055	-0.011
0.127	0.072	-0.916	0.065	0.014	0.011	-0.011
-0.030	-0.117	-0.055	-0.181	-0.124	-0.096	-0.028
0.132	-0.139	-0.013	0.204	0.016	-0.694	0.113
-0.510	0.247	-0.506	-0.143	-0.227	-0.270	0.115
-0.165	0.004	-0.097	0.095	0.079	0.038	0.067
-0.083	-0.308	0.041	-0.313	0.165	-0.008	-0.111
0.021	-0.158	0.037	-0.313	0.113	0.196	0.067
0.095	0.144	0.072	-0.103	0.025	-0.109	0.027
-0.247	-0.511	-0.088	0.137	0.143	0.177	0.266
-0.603	0.246	0.105	-0.044	-0.123	0.259	-0.036
0.064	-0.136	-0.066	0.126	-0.735	0.186	-0.065
0.353	-0.119	0.099	-0.379	-0.083	0.222	0.165
0.470	0.117	-0.039	-0.040	-0.406	0.100	-0.310
0.720	0.182	-0.176	0.184	0.124	-0.011	0.045
-0.171	0.193	-0.029	0.065	-0.173	-0.250	-0.195
0.155	0.080	-0.089	0.048	-0.197	0.126	-0.159
0.257	0.025	-0.101	0.253	-0.320	-0.060	-0.144

TABLE 50--Continued

Variable			Normal Varimax Rotated Factor Loadings		
Number	Name	Communality	1	2	3
37	PCFEMHOUSHLD	0.638	0.598	-0.248	-0.146
38	PCFEMMANFCTG	0.661	0.770	-0.051	-0.080
39	PCFEMCONSTRT	0.738	0.640	0.021	0.090
40	PCNTFEMTRADE	0.812	0.798	-0.123	-0.175
41	PCFEMTRNSPRT	0.569	0.491	0.137	0.087
42	PCFEMSERVICE	0.801	0.858	-0.127	-0.017
43	PCPRIMINDTRY	0.888	0.352	-0.219	-0.758
44	PCSECINDSTRY	0.921	0.155	0.150	0.334
45	PCTERTINDTRY	0.925	-0.288	-0.119	0.140
46	TELPER10000P	0.764	-0.197	0.324	0.123
47	BANKPER50000	0.820	0.222	-0.241	0.063
48	POPPOTENTL61	0.940	-0.137	0.931	0.167
49	ROWCOORDNATS	0.809	0.778	-0.008	-0.076
50	COLCOORDNATS	0.707	-0.219	-0.198	-0.006
51	URBANPOTENTL	0.857	-0.096	0.889	0.141
52	LITRATPOTNTL	0.722	-0.430	0.679	-0.078
53	MFGPOTENTIAL	0.803	-0.018	0.804	0.140

TABLE 50--<u>Continued</u>

Normal Varimax Rotated Factor Loadings						
4	5	6	7	8	9	10
-0.161	0.185	-0.043	0.125	0.038	0.329	0.102
-0.080	0.065	0.035	0.166	-0.077	0.110	0.047
-0.338	0.209	0.124	0.191	-0.299	-0.138	0.026
-0.012	0.002	-0.184	0.090	0.006	-0.255	0.002
-0.186	0.485	-0.069	0.059	-0.040	-0.144	-0.037
-0.100	0.135	-0.015	-0.054	0.075	0.037	0.102
0.004	-0.119	0.083	-0.330	0.096	0.032	-0.041
-0.851	-0.070	-0.002	0.070	0.066	0.132	0.086
0.842	0.141	-0.116	0.085	-0.217	0.036	-0.099
0.360	0.466	-0.391	0.074	0.004	0.183	0.259
0.280	0.361	-0.183	-0.025	0.091	0.606	0.301
-0.094	0.052	0.013	-0.044	-0.011	-0.109	-0.017
-0.030	0.246	0.010	-0.093	0.161	0.181	0.263
0.079	0.018	-0.428	-0.213	0.123	-0.576	-0.193
-0.085	0.080	0.021	-0.135	0.055	-0.023	0.027
-0.069	-0.056	0.059	-0.058	0.065	0.228	0.001
-0.169	0.256	-0.024	-0.126	0.151	0.003	-0.054

COMMENTS ON TABLE 51

1. Numbers 1 to 62 in the column headings correspond to variables as listed in Table 49.

2. The 1's in various columns indicate missing data.

3. In the case of cities like Malegaon, Nagercoil and Alleppey which at present have no railway connections the distances were computed assuming these were railroad centers.

TABLE 51

DATA MATRIX

	1 ('000)	2	3 ('00)	4	5	6	7
Greater Bombay	4152	169.0	245	40	76	663	602
Calcutta	2927	39.7	736	8	25	612	580
Delhi	2323	109.5	212	66	108	781	763
Madras	1729	49.0	353	22	65	901	921
Ahmedabad	1149	35.9	320	37	42	805	766
Hyderabad	1118	72.2	155	9	43	943	990
Bangalore	1093	172.7	63	40	92	876	883
Kanpur	895	104.2	86	38	43	744	700
Nagpur	643	84.0	76	43	49	884	919
Poona	597	50.3	118	24	87	884	865
Lucknow	595	40.0	148	34	25	805	804
Howrah	512	11.1	460	18	14	630	616
Varanasi	485	30.8	157	38	34	853	815
Agra	462	23.9	193	33	30	836	839
Madurai	424	8.6	496	17	51	952	967
Allahabad	413	24.4	169	32	27	797	805
Jaipur	403	25.0	161	39	66	856	895
Indore	394	21.6	183	27	53	851	854
Amritsar	376	13.0	289	16	- 17	802	762
Patna	364	22.3	163	29	44	769	822
Sholapur	337	8.6	391	22	30	902	917
Jamshedpur	303	30.0	101	39	47	787	802
Gwalior	300	24.1	124	24	32	853	898
Baroda	298	10.0	303	41	38	857	862
Jabalpur	295	52.0	56	45	45	846	897
Surat	288	3.2	903	29	30	916	917
Coimbatore	286	8.9	323	45	52	885	890
Bareilly	259	8.8	295	33	8	852	864
Mysore	253	14.4	176	4	62	904	947
Tiruchirapalli	249	8.9	278	14	37	945	957
Salem	249	7.9	315	23	56	957	975
Ludhiana	244	7.6	321	59	38	829	835
Trivandrum	239	17.2	139	28	46	961	955
Ajmer	231	21.5	107	18	34	887	900
Vijayawada	230	9.3	247	43	87	947	957
Jodhpur	224	29.1	77	24	42	847	875
Jullundur	222	17.0	131	32	25	848	853
Merrut	208	7.8	267	32	35	841	816
Rajkot	194	14.0	138	47	99	927	964
Kolhapur	193	27.1	71	41	47	884	918
Calicut	192	11.8	163	21	26	966	982
Guntur	187	11.6	161	49	50	979	987
South Suburb	185	11.7	158	79	64	810	792
Bhopal	185	27.5	67	81	36	807	894
Saharanpur	185	9.8	190	25	41	821	805
Aligarh	185	12.3	150	31	26	825	812
Visakhapatnam	182	11.3	161	69	54	920	978
Gorakhpur	180	15.0	120	36	39	757	777
Moradabad	180	3.8	474	17	8	847	842
Bhavnagar	176	9.1	188	28	34	916	924
Hubli	171	9.4	182	32	36	911	930

TABLE 51--*Continued*

8	9	10 ('00)	11	12	13	14	15	16
586	651	45	540	517	26	10	95	1.4
593	635	147	500	508	24	12	123	1.2
562	634	28	754	504	28	9	78	1.1
595	696	30	1170	493	42	20	121	1.7
527	619	60	527	503	37	16	108	.1
478	588	25	607	533	23	8	49	1.6
501	597	11	562	533	36	13	91	13.7
465	550	14	596	436	22	17	165	11.8
498	620	15	498	487	32	20	19	7.8
550	644	23	518	513	28	10	91	1.3
467	548	29	507	473	30	11	87	.2
517	575	94	488	460	14	12	240	2.8
408	522	16	960	492	32	20	112	.5
364	460	22	867	566	49	11	59	.1
576	702	58	845	483	47	18	91	4.6
477	576	26	641	481	25	8	73	1.4
424	544	29	543	518	17	14	259	10.6
506	615	20	920	494	30	35	129	1.3
527	589	54	534	512	34	11	97	3.5
518	631	23	697	567	11	4	98	1.2
408	545	69	563	533	40	15	81	.6
526	629	18	550	512	21	3	49	2.1
425	543	15	809	506	13	4	27	2.8
554	646	58	525	515	39	15	77	.7
488	594	11	495	468	23	6	76	.7
566	673	126	714	594	37	18	133	3.9
601	704	52	618	498	54	16	85	3.3
388	464	39	746	522	7	3	82	5.7
528	617	29	612	560	32	8	47	7.4
540	656	45	610	481	38	13	57	5.2
446	567	54	581	500	48	17	69	6.6
557	624	62	516	515	35	8	65	.1
617	689	22	640	581	56	12	25	.5
476	593	11	937	514	19	8	73	3.7
504	602	51	483	446	32	14	97	1.2
449	579	11	687	532	8	11	243	32.2
529	608	24	546	544	34	8	53	2.6
435	522	46	582	538	22	5	44	6.2
536	634	24	568	545	29	13	117	3.2
534	660	13	555	550	32	9	42	1.6
544	633	19	827	700	43	19	77	5.9
449	558	28	562	458	40	18	88	4.6
581	650	26	611	572	8	3	137	.1
432	515	12	559	464	21	7	14	5.7
416	500	31	612	494	32	14	99	.7
384	475	18	836	532	14	7	101	4.2
478	589	31	535	506	36	19	129	7.4
494	602	21	555	482	25	7	61	1.8
344	418	58	813	554	35	17	94	2.3
494	598	25	736	530	26	12	82	3.2
491	611	32	566	551	28	7	35	3.2

TABLE 51--Continued

	1 ('000)	2	3 ('00)	4	5	6	7
Warangal	156	24.0	65	17	43	929	954
Gaya	151	11.8	128	13	27	834	854
Bikaner	150	14.7	102	29	- 8	884	935
Jamnagar	148	5.6	250	42	46	914	942
Bhatpara	147	4.6	319	9	15	585	533
Kharagpur	147	12.9	114	14	49	810	909
Kolar Gold Fields	146	30.0	49	- 8	19	984	1004
Cuttack	146	23.0	63	43	38	722	755
Ujjain	144	6.7	213	11	60	872	888
Bhagalpur	143	11.1	129	26	23	817	831
Mangalore	142	8.4	169	22	44	968	992
Jhansi	140	13.6	103	32	21	896	903
Raipur	139	9.7	143	56	42	890	881
Alleppey	138	18.1	76	19	106	984	950
Amravati	137	14.0	98	34	38	852	892
Rampur	135	7.8	178	1	50	850	938
Nasik	131	18.3	71	35	85	924	928
Garden Reach	130	5.0	261	20	28	650	648
Rajahmundry	130	4.1	317	24	41	985	1024
Dehra Dun	129	15.2	85	11	96	827	732
Belgaum	127	3.0	426	26	41	887	915
Kamarhati	125	4.2	296	62	82	648	649
Patiala	125	13.0	96	28	40	798	794
Tuticorin	124	5.2	239	26	31	966	985
Kakinada	122	9.5	129	23	33	971	1002
Ranchi	122	11.4	107	15	71	793	830
Malegaon	121	4.0	301	121	50	893	953
Kota	120	74.7	16	85	38	826	889
Ahmednagar	119	9.5	124	13	50	886	885
Ernakulam	117	10.9	107	89	33	945	897
Mathura	116	3.6	323	19	28	860	860
Akola	115	6.3	183	29	43	854	910
Vellore	113	4.2	272	7	48	980	1002
South Dum Dum	111	6.0	186	81	138	778	702
Udaipur	111	8.6	80	24	50	844	919
Thanjavur	111	8.7	122	10	47	979	1012
Shahjahanpur	110	8.8	302	12	- 6	874	862
Thana	109	8.9	84	61	128	774	779
Muzaffarpur	109	9.0	138	48	36	695	738
Eluru	108	9.1	233	24	34	1004	1044
Burdwan	108	9.2	123	44	20	789	749
Baranagar	107	9.3	392	40	42	762	717
Nellore	106	9.4	202	31	45	932	971
Nagercoil	106	9.5	125	34	53	990	1006
Asansol	103	9.6	258	36	37	664	937
Darbhanga	103	9.7	137	21	23	870	913
Bandar	101	9.8	105	30	32	947	967
Bally	101	9.9	224	60	25	526	533
Kurnool	100	10.0	173	67	33	938	966
Gauhati	100	10.1	183	131	47	497	558
Mirzapur	100	10.2	66	16	22	893	910

TABLE 51--Continued

8	9	10 ('00)	11	12	13	14	15	16
391	531	11	592	495	18	5	16	3.2
444	585	22	578	550	14	14	108	2.4
397	525	17	588	566	19	8	63	2.4
477	590	45	561	552	19	7	30	2.2
504	536	32	441	434	9	10	311	10.8
483	593	23	485	482	3	1	11	2.1
361	473	9	539	534	33	10	73	3.5
534	647	10	619	589	50	17	49	.4
472	597	27	786	465	21	14	109	5.6
444	557	18	725	596	8	7	12	8.9
566	644	27	621	611	35	11	43	2.2
393	514	17	588	494	27	10	108	1.8
471	608	26	542	453	19	4	19	4.9
576	657	12	625	589	26	8	36	.8
514	649	19	502	491	44	13	73	4.6
289	370	23	742	539	6	2	18	1.1
534	662	14	501	497	37	15	121	2.8
420	506	61	429	428	7	5	152	8.2
461	569	39	803	453	33	14	81	2.7
585	648	13	661	468	21	6	56	.3
578	676	57	740	573	20	8	20	4.8
552	592	65	457	456	18	5	34	1.2
536	600	19	510	501	37	17	61	7.6
573	683	50	476	458	34	17	113	9.2
447	540	17	775	481	20	12	89	5.4
582	676	14	755	625	9	6	114	1.5
372	500	51	592	579	29	15	122	3.1
433	561	2	921	454	17	9	123	65.7
538	667	22	571	562	34	12	78	1.7
641	700	16	675	634	23	6	25	1.5
377	540	40	805	506	37	12	76	5.1
483	597	36	502	498	40	11	41	1.7
482	596	32	850	526	58	28	117	4.0
595	651	33	559	555	2	1	6	.1
514	633	14	558	468	10	4	97	.9
532	643	21	626	496	56	17	62	3.5
300	373	45	665	467	31	14	100	1.6
578	645	16	510	504	25	8	62	.8
514	625	19	719	621	25	8	62	.8
481	574	44	527	462	24	13	82	1.4
519	600	22	547	522	13	9	86	21.5
639	689	73	534	512	17	8	147	2.2
514	618	40	496	468	53	21	84	7.4
594	679	22	576	511	34	9	33	3.0
553	629	40	631	589	3	1	6	7.2
398	545	19	722	585	21	12	57	.9
505	577	16	637	509	36	11	61	1.7
525	563	53	420	418	9	5	142	4.5
416	538	29	589	533	38	16	92	4.4
634	672	31	583	530	9	17	471	10.9
370	509	10	625	483	28	10	93	2.1

TABLE 51--Continued

	17	18	19	20	21	22	23
Greater Bombay	10	10	440	305	4	35	41
Calcutta	2	4	950	890	5	43	40
Delhi	40	40	820	580	10	114	31
Madras	80	85	235	220	4	124	31
Ahmedabad	80	60	670	305	7	106	31
Hyderabad	80	80	340	400	4	107	29
Bangalore	35	45	235	220	5	127	32
Kanpur	50	45	260	260	7	154	32
Nagpur	90	100	320	340	7	39	33
Poona	80	75	100	100	4	60	30
Lucknow	50	45	310	300	9	84	30
Howrah	1	1	1	1	6	43	37
Varanasi	30	55	400	400	6	89	32
Agra	35	30	120	120	5	190	27
Madurai	90	95	290	290	4	40	31
Allahabad	50	55	380	360	5	150	30
Jaipur	80	80	180	180	4	100	29
Indore	35	35	240	250	3	101	29
Amritsar	50	45	260	260	6	96	31
Patna	40	55	340	300	6	77	32
Sholapur	145	145	160	190	3	68	33
Jamshedpur	90	80	160	150	3	107	33
Gwalior	55	60	180	180	5	153	29
Baroda	80	60	80	60	4	56	28
Jabalpur	100	160	440	560	3	98	33
Surat	110	75	190	140	5	107	32
Coimbatore	100	95	200	240	3	77	34
Bareilly	45	40	160	150	6	50	28
Mysore	80	80	80	80	3	87	28
Tiruchirapalli	40	30	200	200	5	64	31
Salem	75	95	120	160	4	76	37
Ludhiana	35	30	185	185	6	61	30
Trivandrum	40	138	415	470	1	54	28
Ajmer	80	80	260	220	3	169	26
Vijayawada	18	15	160	210	5	52	34
Jodhpur	130	140	470	320	3	100	27
Jullundur	35	30	210	215	8	166	27
Merrut	40	40	40	40	3	77	29
Rajkot	55	45	200	130	3	36	26
Kolhapur	40	30	240	260	1	78	28
Calicut	100	100	180	350	2	21	28
Guntur	18	15	180	225	4	47	37
South Suburb	2	2	1	6	2	43	28
Bhopal	110	105	340	340	3	54	35
Saharanpur	40	50	100	100	5	65	30
Aligarh	40	50	80	80	3	146	26
Visakhapatnam	90	90	360	410	2	88	30
Gorakhpur	120	135	450	480	4	72	32
Moradabad	15	12	100	100	5	44	28
Bhavnagar	100	120	130	120	2	40	26
Hubli	50	55	240	280	3	64	30

TABLE 51--Continued

24	25	26	27	28	29	30	31	32
9	.3	.1	1.5	1.4	39.5	2.7	18.3	11.2
6	.1	.1	.3	.8	25.2	3.2	23.6	11.7
6	.7	.2	.7	1.7	21.2	4.4	19.6	6.4
10	.1	.1	1.4	2.5	24.5	4.3	19.1	11.8
8	.2	.1	.3	3.0	50.6	2.7	15.5	5.8
18	.7	.7	.9	4.5	15.8	3.5	18.8	10.3
14	5.2	1.3	1.3	4.4	29.5	5.2	13.4	5.2
4	2.9	.8	.6	3.4	35.7	2.5	18.8	8.2
20	2.0	1.4	2.3	16.5	22.2	5.3	14.7	13.6
16	1.5	1.4	1.1	4.5	24.9	4.4	17.3	11.9
7	1.8	.3	.7	3.5	21.3	3.9	18.8	11.5
3	.1	.1	.3	.5	43.3	2.5	19.5	13.2
10	1.7	.3	.6	29.0	11.3	2.4	19.7	8.3
4	1.1	.4	.7	8.3	25.5	3.6	21.2	9.4
16	.4	.4	.7	12.4	28.8	3.0	21.4	7.7
8	1.6	1.1	1.2	4.8	17.3	3.4	17.4	13.3
9	.4	.1	1.1	8.3	18.4	7.0	16.5	8.8
11	.7	.2	1.3	4.1	35.5	3.9	19.6	5.7
4	.4	.6	.7	2.3	31.5	3.0	25.3	10.6
11	5.1	2.2	1.2	5.7	13.1	3.2	14.6	9.6
23	1.1	.7	.8	23.4	38.0	1.9	12.6	6.0
11	.7	.2	1.0	1.4	54.2	6.9	8.3	5.3
9	2.9	1.0	2.3	4.0	30.6	6.2	16.5	6.5
10	1.0	.4	.6	2.6	32.1	2.4	16.6	8.7
17	3.7	1.2	2.1	12.6	20.6	5.6	14.4	13.2
15	.2	.1	.5	17.1	36.3	1.7	16.3	3.8
15	.3	1.2	1.2	7.2	30.1	5.2	19.4	5.9
4	2.2	.3	1.1	6.4	23.2	4.4	19.4	15.1
13	4.0	.4	2.3	4.6	21.8	4.7	16.8	9.4
13	.9	1.8	1.5	7.1	25.4	4.0	21.0	11.7
26	1.2	.7	.7	36.3	18.0	2.1	16.1	4.7
6	.6	.3	.8	6.5	36.2	3.3	19.7	8.4
21	1.2	.7	3.2	2.1	11.6	2.5	14.3	5.9
10	.9	.2	.9	3.4	10.3	5.2	16.4	29.7
16	1.2	1.4	1.6	4.9	17.1	4.2	21.7	18.1
8	.1	.2	4.6	4.2	12.1	7.2	14.6	17.5
5	1.1	.7	.5	3.9	27.2	2.7	20.0	10.4
7	1.8	1.6	1.2	8.4	23.6	3.9	19.4	8.6
12	2.5	.6	.5	4.6	24.6	3.3	17.6	9.3
13	6.5	3.6	1.2	6.2	25.0	2.7	16.5	6.7
15	.4	.1	4.9	3.6	20.4	1.4	16.9	11.2
29	2.2	1.6	.6	3.6	34.8	3.1	15.0	9.9
6	.3	1.0	.5	.7	35.1	4.5	16.7	8.8
13	1.3	.5	2.8	4.6	18.8	13.2	14.0	8.8
4	1.4	.5	1.1	4.1	26.7	2.2	21.3	13.9
6	2.0	.6	.7	6.1	25.1	2.8	20.3	6.0
15	.8	.5	5.0	2.2	11.4	4.0	12.7	21.7
9	1.7	.7	1.1	11.0	17.4	2.0	15.1	21.2
4	1.2	.4	1.3	4.3	34.6	2.1	22.5	9.9
11	.4	.1	.6	3.3	30.4	2.3	17.8	12.6
14	3.0	3.1	.8	8.7	25.5	3.6	16.8	12.3

TABLE 51--Continued

	17	18	19	20	21	22	23
Warangal	80	80	80	80	2	109	35
Gaya	60	55	290	260	5	93	32
Bikaner	140	160	400	280	3	66	26
Jamnagar	55	45	255	175	2	47	28
Bhatpara	14	14	20	22	4	128	38
Kharagpur	70	65	70	65	6	81	29
Kolar Gold Fields	35	45	35	45	2	374	29
Cuttack	180	170	230	240	2	89	36
Ujjain	33	35	360	240	5	118	31
Bhagalpur	35	35	215	230	4	76	30
Mangalore	130	120	220	470	1	28	36
Jhansi	55	60	250	240	4	193	27
Raipur	20	20	460	480	4	50	36
Alleppey	40	40	325	422	2	22	28
Amravati	65	55	280	350	1	43	31
Rampur	15	12	115	112	2	30	29
Nasik	60	75	100	90	4	83	31
Garden Reach	2	2	1	8	2	46	36
Rajahmundry	40	35	240	290	2	77	32
Dehra Dun	40	95	140	195	1	85	30
Belgaum	50	55	300	320	2	27	28
Kamarhati	2	2	8	8	4	48	36
Patiala	20	30	140	150	2	48	29
Tuticorin	30	38	320	380	1	48	32
Kakinada	40	35	280	325	1	73	31
Ranchi	80	90	300	240	2	241	30
Malegaon	60	67	150	157	1	34	41
Kota	105	140	320	285	3	133	33
Ahmednagar	70	90	170	190	2	67	31
Ernakulam	40	110	300	360	2	43	28
Mathura	35	30	85	85	6	77	28
Akola	65	55	300	320	6	34	31
Vellore	80	80	80	80	2	88	31
South Dum Dum	1	2	4	4	5	63	29
Udaipur	165	160	320	400	1	72	32
Thanjavur	40	30	240	230	3	63	31
Shahjahanpur	45	40	205	190	6	55	29
Thana	10	10	10	10	4	49	35
Muzaffarpur	25	60	350	360	3	64	31
Eluru	35	35	195	245	2	71	37
Burdwan	60	60	67	67	5	106	30
Baranagar	1	2	6	6	4	20	31
Nellore	100	100	100	100	2	138	34
Nagercoil	40	40	400	390	1	28	32
Asansol	40	35	120	120	5	63	34
Darbhanga	25	60	340	350	3	87	30
Bandar	40	50	200	260	1	49	31
Bally	5	5	6	7	6	35	43
Kurnool	110	130	110	130	2	99	35
Gauhati	45	45	680	630	2	79	43
Mirzapur	30	55	430	415	4	150	33

TABLE 51--*Continued*

24	25	26	27	28	29	30	31	32
27	5.9	3.5	1.9	14.3	19.7	3.5	14.5	8.2
15	4.1	1.6	1.3	10.8	15.0	3.4	15.7	12.5
10	.3	.3	.3	6.9	9.7	8.2	17.0	16.4
12	2.4	.9	1.3	3.5	24.5	2.1	18.6	9.0
5	.1	.1	.2	.4	70.8	1.2	10.5	4.6
7	.6	1.1	.1	.5	22.8	1.6	13.3	39.7
21	26.8	3.5	40.4	2.0	2.7	1.0	7.8	1.3
8	.9	.2	1.3	9.9	14.7	2.8	13.1	11.6
11	2.5	.9	1.1	4.7	32.2	4.1	17.7	7.9
14	2.4	.5	1.5	24.0	11.6	2.5	15.3	8.4
29	1.2	.6	2.4	5.0	32.5	3.1	14.2	9.4
11	1.3	.5	1.3	8.8	17.8	3.2	16.4	22.1
22	6.7	.7	2.5	6.6	16.3	6.1	19.3	11.9
21	.8	2.9	5.4	7.4	26.4	2.0	16.0	8.8
16	4.2	6.3	1.9	4.4	16.1	3.4	18.6	9.8
5	4.5	1.0	.8	4.4	26.8	4.1	18.4	7.3
20	3.7	4.4	1.3	5.4	23.8	4.2	17.8	7.7
2	.1	.1	.6	7.2	56.0	1.1	12.7	3.8
17	1.1	.4	.8	7.8	19.9	2.5	22.5	15.2
8	.7	.8	2.9	.9	15.4	2.1	18.7	9.0
13	6.9	1.3	.5	11.6	16.8	2.6	19.1	6.6
2	.1	.1	.2	.4	62.8	2.6	12.3	5.6
8	1.9	.5	1.7	4.1	13.7	7.5	17.2	7.0
15	.1	.1	6.2	1.3	31.3	2.9	18.9	17.2
16	1.9	1.4	4.9	5.6	13.9	3.6	18.8	11.9
13	5.4	1.2	2.5	4.2	15.8	4.7	14.9	9.9
32	1.9	1.6	.3	15.3	55.5	1.9	9.9	2.2
13	2.9	1.5	2.2	2.8	11.9	10.7	14.7	15.4
19	2.9	.9	.7	7.3	22.9	2.2	15.1	6.2
18	1.1	1.8	1.6	1.4	17.6	2.4	15.3	8.6
7	1.2	.7	1.1	4.0	15.2	4.1	22.8	9.1
11	3.4	4.3	.9	2.5	19.5	3.5	20.2	12.5
14	.6	.7	.9	8.6	26.4	2.9	20.1	9.0
3	.1	.2	1.9	.8	40.0	1.9	19.8	10.6
14	2.7	.5	1.6	5.2	11.1	11.0	17.6	9.8
18	2.9	4.8	1.7	8.9	15.1	4.3	17.3	8.7
5	4.9	3.0	1.3	6.8	7.9	3.0	20.6	9.0
14	2.2	.9	1.6	1.3	39.8	2.6	13.3	10.5
9	1.7	1.5	1.1	2.4	15.0	4.0	19.9	10.3
23	3.4	4.9	.8	14.0	17.4	2.5	16.9	8.3
9	.7	.4	.6	1.2	16.2	3.7	23.0	15.0
3	.2	.1	.4	.7	47.9	2.9	17.4	6.4
17	3.2	3.6	.8	9.2	15.2	2.5	16.2	10.7
24	5.1	3.2	1.3	19.6	16.0	5.2	15.0	6.6
3	.3	.2	.8	.6	19.7	2.2	22.1	26.0
16	4.2	1.2	2.5	11.1	15.1	2.8	16.6	8.0
16	4.3	5.8	1.9	10.0	14.7	3.0	18.6	10.0
3	.1	.8	.5	.4	63.5	1.5	11.2	8.8
26	2.5	6.1	.8	14.3	14.5	5.9	14.2	6.8
5	.5	.1	.8	2.6	11.3	2.0	14.9	19.8
15	3.2	.8	.8	14.8	16.6	3.4	20.7	7.7

TABLE 51--Continued

	33	34	35	36	37	38	39
Greater Bombay	25.0	39.2	40.7	11.2	28.7	5.0	10.4
Calcutta	35.0	.1	.2	.2	80.4	17.6	11.9
Delhi	45.1	26.0	26.5	15.4	20.7	2.1	6.8
Madras	36.2	1.9	6.2	3.6	30.7	2.7	7.6
Ahmedabad	21.8	13.2	28.3	14.5	34.6	3.7	16.9
Hyderabad	44.8	24.3	54.2	27.4	48.4	9.2	17.5
Bangalore	34.7	27.0	30.2	18.7	38.6	7.7	15.7
Kanpur	27.1	7.3	10.6	5.2	9.0	1.3	2.2
Nagpur	22.0	32.9	54.2	23.7	40.3	8.5	24.0
Poona	33.0	34.2	51.9	17.2	48.5	7.7	9.9
Lucknow	38.2	6.6	21.0	4.8	20.5	2.1	1.6
Howrah	20.5	6.1	.1	2.5	7.4	1.1	1.9
Varanasi	26.7	22.1	29.8	9.5	15.6	3.5	1.6
Agra	29.8	1.3	2.2	2.9	5.5	1.9	1.7
Madurai	25.2	8.7	28.3	9.2	34.1	12.0	17.2
Allahabad	39.9	10.9	33.2	5.5	17.4	3.9	3.8
Jaipur	39.4	23.5	29.9	21.4	29.8	4.1	10.8
Indore	29.0	25.7	29.0	7.8	37.4	4.8	14.5
Amritsar	25.6	.6	2.0	1.2	20.8	1.3	.1
Patna	.6	7.7	3.2	1.1	35.0	6.5	20.5
Sholapur	15.5	13.3	40.1	25.5	42.8	18.1	19.7
Jamshedpur	22.0	29.6	12.4	13.7	27.3	5.4	21.0
Gwalior	30.0	24.3	26.7	8.9	34.4	3.0	4.5
Baroda	35.6	8.0	23.0	23.7	40.2	2.2	13.1
Jabalpur	26.6	33.4	50.1	18.9	35.0	6.5	20.5
Surat	24.0	14.6	29.4	27.7	29.7	8.3	22.9
Coimbatore	29.5	9.9	38.5	12.8	24.0	9.7	26.6
Bareilly	27.9	4.0	.5	1.7	11.6	1.0	.7
Mysore	36.0	16.4	13.0	14.7	38.0	9.8	7.5
Tiruchirapalli	26.6	12.1	40.3	15.0	30.1	5.9	16.0
Salem	20.2	17.3	37.8	22.7	41.2	12.5	24.2
Ludhiana	24.2	2.0	5.3	1.5	24.1	2.1	1.2
Trivandrum	58.5	23.0	30.2	.7	34.9	8.6	3.4
Ajmer	33.0	37.7	28.3	20.4	37.5	7.5	12.5
Vijayawada	29.8	11.7	48.0	26.1	40.5	10.3	16.4
Jodhpur	39.5	16.9	40.2	15.4	20.4	5.3	5.1
Jullundur	33.5	3.7	5.9	1.5	22.0	1.0	.1
Merrut	31.5	6.9	7.1	3.8	28.0	2.6	.9
Rajkot	37.0	32.1	23.9	13.3	38.7	2.9	18.4
Kolhapur	31.6	17.5	33.7	14.7	38.3	3.3	7.6
Calicut	41.1	34.1	46.2	1.1	54.7	13.3	4.1
Guntur	29.2	17.4	32.7	26.4	40.3	51.6	3.5
South Suburb	32.4	2.2	1.0	.7	15.9	6.2	.8
Bhopal	36.0	17.2	37.3	11.4	37.5	5.3	19.3
Saharanpur	28.8	1.6	1.1	5.2	19.3	2.7	.2
Aligarh	36.4	3.1	2.9	2.6	13.6	1.5	1.2
Visakhapatnam	41.7	22.7	14.4	8.8	20.8	3.4	15.8
Gorakhpur	29.8	15.9	24.8	7.8	26.3	1.3	4.1
Moradabad	23.7	1.6	.1	6.5	16.5	.6	.1
Bhavnagar	32.5	23.8	20.0	9.4	40.6	6.0	11.8
Hubli	26.2	14.5	43.0	25.6	30.7	5.6	11.5

TABLE 51--Continued

40	41	42	43	44	45	46	47	48 ('00)
5.6	4.7	16.2	1.9	40.9	57.2	121	2.1	6881
14.9	14.6	13.3	.5	26.0	73.5	266	2.7	6672
1.3	1.8	9.7	1.6	22.9	75.5	250	3.5	4435
5.9	2.7	18.2	1.6	27.0	71.4	123	3.6	3349
5.0	4.9	14.8	.6	53.6	45.8	57	2.9	2659
12.7	1.7	24.1	2.3	20.3	77.4	65	3.0	2578
7.8	1.9	16.9	7.8	33.9	58.3	68	3.5	2525
2.6	.8	9.4	4.3	39.1	56.6	69	2.0	2441
11.0	11.8	19.9	5.7	38.7	55.6	81	2.7	1934
11.0	10.1	21.9	4.0	29.4	66.6	88	5.5	2238
2.9	.7	11.8	2.8	24.8	72.4	98	1.7	2052
1.7	.7	9.8	.5	43.8	55.7	40	1.0	6666
5.6	.8	13.7	2.6	40.3	57.1	47	1.8	1748
1.5	.4	8.4	2.2	33.8	64.0	72	2.4	2001
8.2	2.2	21.3	1.5	41.2	57.3	52	4.0	1604
5.7	.8	12.2	3.9	22.1	74.0	64	1.8	1701
2.8	.8	11.7	1.6	26.7	71.7	70	3.3	1760
4.8	1.4	18.4	2.2	39.6	58.2	57	2.3	1767
.5	.4	11.8	1.7	33.8	64.5	77	4.4	1350
9.2	1.2	21.4	7.0	33.2	59.8	40	2.0	1467
10.2	3.7	21.7	2.6	61.4	36.0	21	2.5	1673
6.7	4.5	23.4	1.9	55.6	42.5	21	1.2	1517
5.5	1.2	14.2	6.2	34.6	49.2	34	1.8	1757
7.4	1.4	17.6	2.0	34.7	63.3	48	3.2	1764
9.2	1.2	21.4	7.0	33.2	59.8	40	2.0	1467
7.0	1.7	23.3	.8	53.4	45.8	60	2.6	1755
7.8	3.2	23.4	2.7	37.3	60.0	106	7.3	1522
1.3	.1	10.8	3.6	29.6	66.8	29	3.0	1643
11.5	.9	16.3	6.7	26.4	66.9	40	3.9	1454
6.3	2.4	22.2	4.2	32.5	63.3	43	5.8	1431
12.5	.8	25.6	2.6	54.3	43.1	44	5.0	1479
.6	.4	14.4	1.7	42.7	55.6	46	3.3	1440
14.9	5.1	26.7	5.1	13.7	81.2	108	5.6	1100
3.3	.7	16.7	2.0	13.7	84.3	28	1.7	1421
12.0	2.1	22.5	4.2	22.0	73.8	67	4.3	1543
3.7	.5	13.6	4.9	16.3	78.8	38	2.4	1271
.4	.7	10.9	2.3	31.1	66.6	94	3.6	1297
1.4	.3	10.8	4.6	32.0	63.4	79	2.9	1837
2.6	1.1	20.3	3.6	29.2	67.2	53	3.6	1315
8.1	.9	17.5	11.3	31.2	57.5	40	6.2	1491
1.3	2.3	23.6	5.4	24.0	70.6	98	7.3	1155
10.7	1.0	23.9	4.4	38.4	57.2	45	2.9	1580
1.4	1.3	12.7	1.8	35.8	62.4	8	.8	5195
4.5	1.1	14.2	4.6	23.4	72.0	79	2.2	1356
.2	.1	9.4	3.0	30.8	66.2	25	1.9	1599
3.1	1.9	10.9	3.3	31.2	65.5	31	1.9	1836
28.4	1.7	19.4	6.3	13.6	80.1	52	2.5	1187
7.4	.4	15.3	3.5	28.4	68.1	32	3.6	1335
1.1	.1	10.1	2.9	38.9	58.2	27	2.5	1624
3.1	1.6	18.4	1.1	33.7	65.2	43	2.8	1517
8.9	1.3	18.9	6.9	34.2	58.9	31	4.7	1262

TABLE 51--Continued

	33	34	35	36	37	38	39
Warangal	28.5	36.1	67.2	17.0	50.1	22.0	21.0
Gaya	35.6	22.6	42.7	14.2	39.9	7.1	3.0
Bikaner	40.9	21.8	82.4	14.9	27.5	11.5	7.3
Jamnagar	37.7	26.7	32.0	13.1	44.2	6.8	12.6
Bhatpara	12.6	16.7	.1	7.0	20.3	3.5	5.1
Kharagpur	20.3	15.4	32.7	13.6	16.5	1.6	7.6
Kolar Gold Fields	14.5	43.4	44.6	3.8	37.6	5.9	10.7
Cuttack	45.5	.9	2.0	2.8	16.8	2.8	.2
Ujjain	28.9	26.9	44.1	12.9	37.5	6.5	13.9
Bhagalpur	33.8	11.5	10.1	9.1	31.9	5.3	2.1
Mangalore	31.6	45.1	63.6	42.0	69.2	37.4	10.9
Jhansi	28.6	22.8	22.4	11.4	27.4	9.4	2.8
Raipur	29.9	42.9	58.0	17.2	39.5	13.8	18.1
Alleppey	30.3	7.6	57.4	3.8	83.0	14.4	7.9
Amravati	35.3	16.2	49.6	31.7	34.1	12.5	13.8
Rampur	32.7	12.3	2.5	7.0	16.6	1.7	.5
Nasik	31.7	31.5	54.9	11.1	37.8	18.5	16.5
Garden Reach	18.4	.1	2.4	1.0	1.0	1.6	1.4
Rajahmundry	29.8	13.8	28.1	9.9	30.7	19.3	17.4
Dehra Dun	49.5	12.5	14.8	2.2	28.1	3.0	11.6
Belgaum	34.6	30.2	70.7	14.4	28.7	4.7	3.1
Kamarhati	15.6	.1	.1	12.2	27.3	1.6	2.8
Patiala	46.4	2.6	14.6	3.6	30.8	3.3	1.2
Tuticorin	22.0	23.1	5.9	2.3	62.6	19.8	17.9
Kakinada	38.0	9.2	37.8	6.0	27.1	8.8	16.2
Ranchi	41.4	40.4	41.1	7.6	20.3	4.8	15.1
Malegaon	11.4	31.9	61.6	22.7	62.4	32.3	25.4
Kota	37.9	18.4	61.9	17.3	43.4	10.9	8.6
Ahmednagar	41.8	31.6	43.8	13.1	30.6	30.8	14.0
Ernakulam	50.2	27.0	47.7	4.3	35.8	4.7	2.4
Mathura	41.8	12.1	3.6	5.2	19.5	3.1	.3
Akola	33.2	14.6	55.7	16.2	28.3	8.2	8.6
Vellore	30.8	4.5	30.6	12.7	54.8	3.1	8.2
South Dum Dum	24.7	3.4	.1	1.5	32.5	2.0	1.8
Udaipur	40.5	37.2	28.0	29.2	46.3	5.1	17.3
Thanjavur	36.3	16.0	45.2	9.3	44.9	7.0	7.3
Shahjahanpur	43.5	3.2	1.7	2.4	12.7	2.1	.3
Thana	27.8	44.7	33.7	25.9	27.3	6.3	17.8
Muzaffarpur	44.1	10.4	2.7	9.5	19.0	2.8	.7
Eluru	31.9	19.3	60.7	8.3	45.4	11.1	15.1
Burdwan	39.2	16.2	1.4	5.8	29.5	9.4	3.6
Baranagar	24.0	.1	.1	3.7	10.8	1.2	2.8
Nellore	38.6	14.7	45.1	7.8	37.3	5.2	9.4
Nagercoil	28.0	11.0	39.4	4.9	61.2	10.0	.6
Asansol	28.1	.1	1.1	.6	10.0	.6	1.0
Darbhanga	38.5	18.2	11.6	6.0	45.7	5.3	5.2
Bandar	31.7	13.7	44.1	3.9	32.4	4.5	18.2
Bally	13.2	.1	16.2	1.0	16.3	1.2	2.4
Kurnool	34.9	27.8	59.3	18.6	58.9	13.4	19.4
Gauhati	48.0	2.3	.1	10.7	65.1	1.5	.1
Mirzapur	32.0	27.2	39.6	10.4	19.8	4.6	2.0

TABLE 51--Continued

40	41	42	43	44	45	46	47	48 ('00)
19.0	2.5	25.2	11.3	34.0	54.7	11	1.6	1377
6.5	.3	18.1	7.0	25.8	67.2	25	2.0	1402
3.4	.3	12.4	.9	16.6	82.5	29	3.0	1132
2.6	.8	16.2	4.6	28.0	67.4	45	4.7	1161
3.3	.5	12.9	.4	71.2	28.4	1	1.0	3010
3.3	4.6	16.3	1.8	23.3	74.9	9	1.0	1865
18.8	.2	26.3	70.7	4.7	24.6	6	0.7	1529
3.4	1.5	19.3	2.4	24.6	73.0	77	3.1	1201
5.0	2.8	19.5	4.5	36.9	58.6	34	2.8	1487
6.6	2.2	13.6	4.4	35.6	60.0	21	1.7	1316
12.3	1.1	30.7	4.2	37.5	58.3	71	9.5	1040
10.3	.8	16.8	3.1	26.6	70.3	23	2.5	1371
13.5	4.5	30.9	9.9	22.9	67.2	48	2.5	1304
6.7	5.6	26.4	9.1	33.8	57.1	59	11.2	1172
4.4	.8	18.4	12.4	20.5	67.1	43	2.9	1409
.8	.1	7.2	6.3	31.2	62.5	16	1.1	1621
12.0	5.8	23.5	9.4	29.2	61.4	30	2.7	1579
1.1	1.8	4.8	.8	63.2	36.0	9	.8	6666
14.0	5.2	22.9	2.3	27.7	70.0	32	2.6	1233
1.2	.7	12.4	4.4	16.3	79.3	88	5.0	1296
6.8	.8	13.1	8.7	28.4	62.9	50	8.2	1212
1.0	.8	10.8	.4	63.2	36.4	2	.8	6433
.6	.5	11.6	4.1	17.8	78.1	38	4.0	1429
8.7	1.7	25.9	6.4	32.6	61.0	46	6.4	1022
15.3	1.9	24.7	8.2	19.5	72.3	31	3.7	1179
4.5	2.2	17.1	9.1	20.0	70.9	62	2.5	1227
9.4	3.8	17.3	3.8	70.8	25.4	2	1.2	1544
9.9	1.1	15.4	6.6	14.7	78.7	28	3.7	1316
8.3	6.8	15.4	4.5	30.2	65.3	23	2.5	1557
5.2	5.4	26.3	4.5	19.0	76.5	125	11.5	1069
3.0	.7	11.1	3.0	19.2	77.8	28	2.6	1657
4.6	1.6	16.9	8.6	22.0	69.4	62	4.8	1387
5.5	3.7	22.2	2.2	35.0	62.8	46	4.4	1306
1.3	1.2	10.9	2.2	40.8	57.0	42	.4	6433
12.0	.8	17.0	4.8	16.3	78.9	29	2.2	1242
9.1	3.0	21.8	9.4	24.0	66.6	24	5.4	1280
1.5	.1	7.6	9.2	14.7	76.1	27	3.2	1413
10.3	6.8	21.4	4.7	41.1	54.2	37	.9	3737
4.5	.3	12.9	4.3	17.4	78.3	60	3.2	1312
14.1	5.1	27.2	9.1	31.3	59.6	30	2.8	1267
2.1	1.5	16.2	1.7	17.4	80.9	26	2.3	2162
.8	1.2	14.2	.7	48.6	50.7	9	.9	6433
11.8	.6	23.2	7.6	24.4	68.0	35	3.3	1251
6.4	.1	22.4	9.6	35.6	54.8	27	5.6	987
.8	.6	8.3	1.3	20.3	78.4	81	4.4	1331
16.3	.4	16.1	7.9	26.2	65.9	20	2.6	1217
12.4	2.7	21.6	12.0	24.7	63.3	21	3.0	1263
1.5	.8	11.6	1.4	63.9	34.7	4	.8	5489
15.2	2.0	21.9	9.4	28.8	61.8	24	3.0	1292
1.9	1.9	5.8	1.4	13.9	84.7	115	6.0	821
12.8	.2	20.3	4.8	31.4	63.8	25	2.5	1434

TABLE 51--Continued

	49	50	51 ('00)	52 ('00)	53 ('00)	54
Greater Bombay	175	43	1255	312	1896	64.2
Calcutta	143	183	1962	517	2213	52.6
Delhi	85	83	563	286	436	56.2
Madras	236	110	545	253	481	37.2
Ahmedabad	138	42	271	203	298	50.8
Hyderabad	194	93	275	190	225	29.8
Bangalore	237	84	282	187	270	47.1
Kanpur	107	112	279	235	258	53.7
Nagpur	157	100	242	214	218	45.4
Poona	182	51	269	188	288	51.7
Lucknow	103	117	279	239	233	47.2
Howrah	143	182	540	251	822	54.2
Varanasi	118	135	236	211	211	30.7
Agra	100	92	281	235	249	35.9
Madurai	267	88	235	171	241	33.6
Allahabad	117	124	227	212	200	35.1
Jaipur	101	73	225	198	183	36.2
Indore	141	71	250	236	227	44.5
Amritsar	55	66	195	192	181	49.2
Patna	115	153	228	192	214	41.5
Sholapur	191	70	209	179	210	39.2
Jamshedpur	142	163	207	179	239	59.1
Gwalior	108	93	243	236	208	37.3
Baroda	145	47	241	216	236	44.3
Jabalpur	138	108	222	212	205	59.6
Surat	155	44	241	197	255	28.8
Coimbatore	256	77	240	181	266	44.4
Bareilly	89	104	242	218	205	37.1
Mysore	244	75	226	186	227	32.4
Tiruchirapalli	259	94	225	161	228	38.8
Salem	250	89	232	166	230	27.4
Ludhiana	63	74	219	235	199	65.1
Trivandrum	281	76	210	208	242	33.1
Admer	105	62	210	193	172	48.5
Vijayawada	203	113	217	173	194	61.7
Jodhpur	106	48	167	155	142	26.8
Jullundur	59	72	218	239	198	62.6
Merrut	82	90	299	231	259	43.3
Rajkot	143	26	203	171	189	45.3
Kolhapur	191	54	209	179	210	39.9
Calicut	253	66	220	200	251	25.5
Guntur	205	113	216	166	198	51.3
South Suburb	144	182	441	199	583	59.4
Rhopal	137	85	223	216	199	64.3
Saharanpur	72	89	240	223	204	38.4
Aligarh	93	93	270	233	231	37.3
Visakhapatnam	191	137	184	151	169	42.8
Gorankhpur	104	138	193	190	185	43.3
Moradabad	83	98	260	220	219	25.0
Bhavnagar	149	38	215	181	208	32.4
Hubli	212	61	212	180	194	38.6

TABLE 51--Continued

55	56	57	58	59	60	61	62
35.5	15.0	51.4	29.4	4.1	57.7	32.8	9.5
30.8	14.2	48.5	32.8	4.3	48.9	14.9	36.1
43.4	19.4	48.5	26.4	5.7	48.3	34.2	17.4
45.7	15.6	48.3	30.2	5.9	52.9	41.8	5.2
43.0	18.6	46.2	30.7	4.4	67.5	28.0	4.5
45.9	20.7	48.8	25.8	4.7	64.9	31.8	3.2
46.0	18.7	48.0	27.4	5.9	52.5	43.5	4.0
41.1	19.1	44.3	30.9	5.7	66.2	27.0	6.8
47.2	15.0	45.8	31.2	7.7	56.6	36.9	6.5
47.1	19.0	44.9	29.9	6.1	54.2	40.3	5.5
42.5	18.2	47.5	28.2	6.0	55.9	31.7	12.4
33.8	16.1	49.2	30.3	4.4	62.2	19.8	17.9
46.4	19.6	41.8	29.4	9.1	59.9	32.9	7.2
48.8	27.7	38.4	26.2	7.6	44.7	42.0	15.3
48.2	15.4	46.0	33.5	5.1	64.8	33.1	2.1
43.4	19.4	42.6	33.3	4.6	58.1	34.7	7.2
46.9	19.3	47.5	26.9	6.2	41.8	33.3	24.9
47.4	16.0	45.1	31.6	7.3	43.2	43.1	13.7
42.7	14.4	49.2	29.0	7.3	36.4	15.8	47.8
43.0	17.2	50.4	26.8	5.5	67.1	24.5	8.4
48.5	18.2	42.5	32.0	7.2	66.1	31.2	2.7
42.5	19.1	43.9	32.5	4.4	66.3	21.7	12.0
47.3	14.9	48.3	29.8	6.9	44.5	36.7	18.8
46.2	19.7	48.0	26.9	5.4	56.0	33.5	10.5
44.3	17.6	47.7	29.4	5.3	46.8	40.7	12.5
45.8	18.5	45.9	29.3	6.4	61.8	33.0	5.2
45.2	17.4	47.8	29.2	5.5	59.4	38.1	2.5
41.0	16.1	47.9	31.2	4.8	34.0	31.6	34.4
48.8	20.7	46.3	26.4	6.5	45.5	48.5	6.0
50.5	18.5	47.0	29.1	5.3	56.9	38.7	4.4
48.7	19.7	45.7	29.3	5.2	69.7	28.7	1.6
44.7	17.5	50.0	25.6	6.8	29.8	19.3	50.9
48.2	17.2	46.4	30.1	6.2	70.1	26.9	3.0
50.0	23.4	42.5	26.4	6.8	34.2	33.5	32.3
47.9	25.3	45.2	23.6	5.4	73.6	25.1	1.3
45.0	28.3	44.0	22.3	5.3	42.6	32.4	25.0
46.2	15.8	49.8	27.0	7.3	27.4	17.5	55.1
19.7	48.8	24.9	6.5	47.1	34.0	47.1	18.9
51.1	21.2	45.3	28.1	6.2	49.3	40.2	10.5
50.0	19.7	44.0	29.5	6.0	68.6	29.8	1.5
46.9	15.5	41.8	34.5	8.1	69.0	27.7	3.2
52.1	20.3	48.2	25.2	6.1	83.0	16.5	.5
46.8	31.0	41.5	22.5	5.0	34.9	24.5	40.6
41.2	22.0	51.3	22.3	4.5	33.5	48.9	17.6
54.9	18.3	44.5	28.3	8.7	34.4	30.3	35.3
46.3	20.8	44.0	28.4	6.5	36.9	30.0	33.1
47.7	21.8	48.4	25.7	3.9	58.6	34.9	6.5
41.1	19.5	51.0	25.0	4.7	69.9	21.0	9.1
53.3	18.4	47.9	28.2	5.2	33.4	49.9	16.7
50.0	23.3	42.4	27.5	6.8	51.9	35.9	12.2
48.5	22.9	43.8	27.1	6.1	52.1	43.3	4.6

TABLE 51--Continued

	49	50	51 ('00)	52 ('00)	53 ('00)	54
Warangal	188	103	206	173	195	34.0
Gaya	122	152	206	185	201	35.8
Bikaner	90	51	160	151	134	24.0
Jamnagar	141	20	173	150	162	35.9
Bhatpara	140	183	441	199	583	61.2
Kharagpur	146	174	244	178	304	44.9
Kolar Gold Fields	235	89	238	177	215	32.2
Cuttack	164	161	171	163	178	36.9
Ujjain	137	71	226	220	203	44.4
Bhagalpur	118	170	199	180	204	31.4
Mangalore	237	57	189	174	204	33.8
Jhansi	116	96	227	223	192	51.4
Raipur	157	123	187	174	179	58.4
Alleppey	271	71	211	240	280	26.1
Amravati	159	88	226	214	200	52.7
Rampur	84	101	239	222	203	14.8
Nasik	167	52	246	193	260	50.4
Garden Reach	143	182	441	199	583	39.2
Rajahmundry	198	124	203	164	185	46.1
Dehra Dun	69	93	210	234	174	75.3
Belgaum	208	56	210	179	200	41.5
Kamarhati	142	183	441	199	583	52.8
Patiala	68	79	216	219	180	60.0
Tuticorin	278	88	200	162	211	44.3
Kakinada	199	128	203	164	185	41.8
Ranchi	136	156	194	177	202	41.8
Malegaon	162	59	246	193	260	44.6
Kota	119	72	209	205	180	49.1
Ahmednagar	176	60	239	190	251	45.5
Ernakulam	266	71	220	228	280	36.0
Mathura	96	89	266	235	221	43.7
Akola	161	81	226	211	202	53.9
Vellore	238	99	237	166	225	35.9
South Dum Dum	142	183	441	199	583	67.5
Udaipur	123	53	192	182	170	34.2
Thanjavur	259	98	208	150	199	41.4
Shahjahanpur	92	108	228	214	192	30.0
Thana	174	43	297	192	356	63.5
Muzaffarpur	110	155	190	177	181	49.5
Eluru	201	119	209	173	189	47.2
Burdwan	137	178	316	199	434	50.9
Baranagar	143	183	441	199	583	57.1
Nellore	223	107	198	157	181	40.5
Nagercoil	284	81	180	203	196	27.3
Asansol	133	170	316	199	434	49.5
Darbhanga	109	160	186	171	182	33.0
Bandar	206	118	217	173	194	37.6
Bally	142	182	540	251	822	72.3
Kurnool	209	89	210	168	187	38.0
Gauhati	107	212	126	138	124	61.0
Mirzapur	120	130	202	194	190	27.0

TABLE 51--Continued

55	56	57	58	59	60	61	62
56.6	26.1	40.8	27.8	5.3	73.4	25.7	.9
50.0	17.7	44.4	30.2	7.9	76.2	16.0	7.8
47.2	25.4	43.6	25.1	5.8	43.4	42.5	14.1
49.0	19.9	49.9	25.5	4.5	45.3	36.8	17.9
30.0	21.4	45.4	29.2	3.9	58.8	17.8	23.4
47.7	22.6	47.1	26.0	3.8	58.2	26.8	15.0
55.5	15.7	44.9	31.3	8.4	67.0	31.1	1.9
42.6	34.0	43.5	16.2	6.2	63.2	28.5	8.3
48.4	15.6	44.5	31.5	7.4	40.0	48.6	1.4
48.9	16.5	46.3	30.0	7.0	66.3	19.6	14.1
47.9	17.6	41.9	32.3	8.4	73.3	24.5	2.2
47.2	30.2	45.9	20.1	3.6	41.0	54.6	4.4
46.9	19.1	48.0	27.3	5.4	55.4	34.0	10.6
52.8	16.4	37.5	37.5	8.3	68.9	28.3	2.8
47.2	17.3	47.2	27.8	7.5	58.2	33.6	8.2
48.0	16.6	45.4	30.7	7.1	41.0	40.5	18.5
50.0	21.2	44.0	28.0	6.8	53.7	39.2	7.1
21.5	17.9	45.3	32.6	3.7	60.5	25.0	14.5
51.6	24.3	43.6	25.8	5.9	74.6	23.8	1.6
45.4	23.9	43.7	25.0	7.3	32.2	28.6	39.2
45.3	26.6	46.8	22.7	3.5	52.6	39.3	8.1
37.8	28.9	40.9	26.8	3.2	45.8	27.9	26.3
44.0	17.5	49.1	26.1	7.0	36.1	24.4	39.5
50.9	17.3	39.8	35.8	7.2	79.3	18.4	2.3
51.9	24.7	44.6	24.9	5.7	70.7	27.2	2.1
41.2	24.0	48.9	21.8	5.0	56.1	33.7	10.2
46.3	23.8	46.4	23.6	6.0	57.5	39.9	2.6
46.6	26.5	39.2	28.3	6.0	53.0	32.4	14.6
48.1	21.1	45.4	27.4	6.0	63.4	28.9	7.7
52.4	18.1	46.1	30.1	5.9	62.6	34.3	3.1
51.0	16.7	46.6	28.8	7.7	48.2	40.0	11.7
43.4	18.0	45.8	29.1	7.1	52.4	41.2	6.4
56.1	18.0	44.8	30.4	6.5	56.2	41.2	2.6
42.6	23.5	45.6	26.4	4.3	20.1	18.5	61.4
46.1	16.8	50.5	27.2	5.2	56.2	24.9	18.9
53.7	21.1	42.2	29.8	6.7	53.0	44.5	2.5
51.5	18.6	42.6	32.2	6.3	50.7	37.4	11.9
42.3	21.8	50.0	24.1	3.8	47.9	44.1	8.0
38.9	19.4	47.4	27.7	5.4	71.9	18.2	9.9
58.4	28.0	40.4	26.3	5.3	72.4	26.8	.8
44.5	34.0	32.8	28.6	4.4	50.8	21.3	27.9
37.7	30.3	40.8	24.8	3.9	34.7	44.0	21.3
47.7	19.9	45.6	28.0	6.2	74.1	25.7	.2
51.5	19.0	42.4	30.1	8.0	77.6	19.6	2.8
33.3	23.5	48.7	24.4	3.3	48.0	28.1	23.9
50.0	16.1	50.9	27.3	3.1	77.3	14.8	7.9
55.8	16.6	46.6	28.9	10.4	77.8	19.5	2.7
29.1	23.2	48.7	26.8	1.1	51.1	29.1	19.8
49.1	24.8	47.5	22.7	5.0	79.7	18.5	1.8
27.8	27.6	49.0	21.2	2.1	43.0	29.4	27.6
61.1	17.8	40.4	32.9	8.6	66.6	31.8	1.6

SELECTED BIBLIOGRAPHY

Books

Davis, K. The Population of India and Pakistan. Princeton: Princeton University Press, 1951.

Duncan, O. D. et al. Metropolis and Region. Baltimore: John Hopkins Press; Published for Resources for the Future, 1960.

Harman, H. H. Modern Factor Analysis. Chicago: University of Chicago Press, 1961.

Hauser, P. M. (ed.). Urbanization in Asia and the Far East. Proceedings of the Joint UN/Unesco Seminar on Urbanization in the ECAFE region, Bangkok, 8-18 August, 1956. Calcutta: Unesco Research Center, 1957.

Kendall, M. G. A Course in Multivariate Analysis. London: Charles Griffin, 1957.

Moser, C. A. and Scott, W. British Towns: A Statistical Study of Their Social and Economic Differences. Center for Urban Studies, Report No. 2. Edinburgh: Oliver and Boyd, 1961.

Pitts, F. R. (ed.). Urban Systems and Economic Development. Eugene: University of Oregon, 1962.

Turner, R. (ed.). India's Urban Future. Berkeley: University of California Press, 1962.

Articles and Unpublished Materials

Berry, B. J. L. and Garrison, W. L. "Alternate Explanations of Urban Rank-Size Relationships," Annals of the Association of American Geographers, XLVIII (March, 1958), 83-91.

Berry, B. J. L. "Cities as Systems within Systems of Cities," in Friedmann, John and Alonso, William (eds.). Regional Development and Planning. Cambridge: M.I.T. Press, 1964.

________. "City Size Distributions and Economic Development," Economic Development and Cultural Change, IX (July, 1961), 573-87.

________. "A Note Concerning Methods of Classification," Annals of the Association of American Geographers, XLVIII (September, 1958), 300-303.

________. "A Method for Deriving Multifactor Uniform Regions," Przeglad Geograficzny (Polish Geographical Review), XXXIII, No. 2 (1961), 263-79.

Ginsburg, N. S. "Urban Geography and 'Non-Western' Areas," in Hauser, P. and Schnore, L. F. (eds.). The Study of Urbanization. New York: John Wiley and Sons, Inc., 1965.

Harris, B. "Urbanization Policy in India," Papers and Proceedings, The Regional Science Association, V (1959), 181-203.

Hoselitz, B. F. "Generative and Parasitic Cities," Economic Development and Cultural Change, III (April, 1955), 278-94.

Kar, N. R. "Economic Character of Metropolitan Sphere of Influence of Calcutta," Geographical Review of India, XXV (June, 1963), 108-137.

Lal, A. "Some Characteristics of Indian Cities of Over 100,000 Inhabitants in 1951, with Special Reference to Their Occupational Structure and Functional Specialization." Unpublished Ph.D. dissertation, Department of Geography, Indiana University, 1958.

________. "Age and Sex Structure of Cities of India," Geographical Review of India, XXIV (March, 1962), 7-29.

Mitra, S. "The Future of Population, Urbanization, and Working Force in India." Unpublished Ph.D. dissertation, Department of Sociology, University of Chicago, 1961.

Ray, M. and Berry, B. J. L. "Multivariate Socio-Economic Regionalization: A Pilot Study in Central Canada." Forthcoming in Ostry, S. and Rymes, T. (eds.). Regional Statistical Studies. Toronto: University of Toronto Press, 1965.

Redfield, R. and Singer, M. "The Cultural Role of Cities," Economic Development and Cultural Change, III (October, 1954), 53-73.

Sources of Data

The Registrar General, India. Vital Statistics of India for 1960. New Delhi: Ministry of Home Affairs, 1962.

The Indian Export Trade Journal. The All India Telephone Directory. Fourth edition. Parts I, II and III. Baroda: Indian Export Trade Journal, 1962.

Mitra, A. Census of India 1961. Vol. I. India. Part II-A (i). Delhi: Manager of Publications, 1963.

________. Census of India 1961. Vol. I. India. Part II-A (ii). Delhi: Manager of Publications, 1963.

THE UNIVERSITY OF CHICAGO
DEPARTMENT OF GEOGRAPHY
RESEARCH PAPERS (Planographed, 6 × 9 Inches)

(Available from Department of Geography, Rosenwald Hall, The University of Chicago, Chicago, Illinois, 60637. Price: four dollars each; by series subscription, three dollars each.)

*1. GROSS, HERBERT HENRY. *Educational Land Use in the River Forest–Oak Park Community (Illinois)*
*2. EISEN, EDNA E. *Educational Land Use in Lake County, Ohio*
*3. WEIGEND, GUIDO GUSTAV. *The Cultural Pattern of South Tyrol (Italy)*
*4. NELSON, HOWARD JOSEPH, *The Livelihood Structure of Des Moines, Iowa*
*5. MATTHEWS, JAMES SWINTON. *Expressions of Urbanism in the Sequent Occupance of Northeastern Ohio*
*6. GINSBURG, NORTON SYDNEY. *Japanese Prewar Trade and Shipping in the Oriental Triangle*
*7. KEMLER, JOHN H. *The Struggle for Wolfram in the Iberian Peninsula, June, 1942—June, 1944: A Study in Political and Economic Geography in Wartime*
*8. PHILBRICK, ALLEN K. *The Geography of Education in the Winnetka and Bridgeport Communities of Metropolitan Chicago*
*9. BRADLEY, VIRGINIA. *Functional Patterns in the Guadalupe Counties of the Edwards Plateau*
*10. HARRIS, CHAUNCY D., and FELLMANN, JEROME DONALD. *A Union List of Geographical Serials*
*11. DE MEIRLEIR, MARCEL J. *Manufactural Occupance in the West Central Area of Chicago*
*12. FELLMANN, JEROME DONALD. *Truck Transportation Patterns of Chicago*
*13. HOTCHKISS, WESLEY AKIN. *Areal Pattern of Religious Institutions in Cincinnati*
*14. HARPER, ROBERT ALEXANDER. *Recreational Occupance of the Moraine Lake Region of Northeastern Illinois and Southeastern Wisconsin*
*15. WHEELER, JESSE HARRISON, JR. *Land Use in Greenbrier County, West Virginia*
*16. MCGAUGH, MAURICE EDRON. *The Settlement of the Saginaw Basin*
*17. WATTERSON, ARTHUR WELDON. *Economy and Land Use Patterns of McLean County, Illinois*
*18. HORBALY, WILLIAM. *Agricultural Conditions in Czechoslovakia, 1950*
*19. GUEST, BUDDY ROSS. *Resource Use and Associated Problems in the Upper Cimarron Area*
*20. SORENSEN, CLARENCE WOODROW. *The Internal Structure of the Springfield, Illinois, Urbanized Area*
*21. MUNGER, EDWIN S. *Relational Patterns of Kampala, Uganda*
*22. KHALAF, JASSIM M. *The Water Resources of the Lower Colorado River Basin*
*23. GULICK, LUTHER H. *Rural Occupance in Utuado and Jayuya Municipios, Puerto Rico*
*24. TAAFFE, EDWARD JAMES. *The Air Passenger Hinterland of Chicago*
*25. KRAUSE, ANNEMARIE ELISABETH. *Mennonite Settlement in the Paraguayan Chaco*
*26. HAMMING, EDWARD. *The Port of Milwaukee*
*27. CRAMER, ROBERT ELI. *Manufacturing Structure of the Cicero District, Metropolitan Chicago*
*28. PIERSON, WILLIAM H. *The Geography of the Bellingham Lowland, Washington*
*29. WHITE, GILBERT F. *Human Adjustment to Floods: A Geographical Approach to the Flood Problem in the United States*
30. OSBORN, DAVID G. *Geographical Features of the Automation of Industry* 1953. 120 pp.
*31. THOMAN, RICHARD S. *The Changing Occupance Pattern of the Tri-State Area, Missouri, Kansas, and Oklahoma*
*32. ERICKSEN, SHELDON D. *Occupance in the Upper Deschutes Basin, Oregon*
*33. KENYON, JAMES B. *The Industrialization of the Skokie Area*
*34. PHILLIPS, PAUL GROUNDS. *The Hashemite Kingdom of Jordan: Prolegomena to a Technical Assistance Program*
*35. CARMIN, ROBERT LEIGHTON. *Anápolis, Brazil: Regional Capital of an Agricultural Frontier*
36. GOLD, ROBERT N. *Manufacturing Structure and Pattern of the South Bend–Mishawaka Area* 1954. 224 pp. 6 folded inserts. 2 maps in pocket.
*37. SISCO, PAUL HARDEMAN. *The Retail Function of Memphis*
*38. VAN DONGEN, IRENE S. *The British East African Transport Complex*
*39. FRIEDMANN, JOHN R. P. *The Spatial Structure of Economic Development in the Tennessee Valley*
*40. GROTEWOLD, ANDREAS. *Regional Changes in Corn Production in the United States from 1909 to 1949*
*41. BJORKLUND, E. M. *Focus on Adelaide—Functional Organization of the Adelaide Region, Australia*
*42. FORD, ROBERT N. *A Resource Use Analysis and Evaluation of the Everglades Agricultural Area*
*43. CHRISTENSEN, DAVID E. *Rural Occupance in Transition: Sumter and Lee Counties, Georgia*
*44. GUZMÁN, LOUIS E. *Farming and Farmlands in Panama*

* Out of print.

*45. ZADROZNY, MITCHELL G. *Water Utilization in the Middle Mississippi Valley*

*46. AHMED, G. MUNIR. *Manufacturing Structure and Pattern of Waukegan–North Chicago*

47. RANDALL, DARRELL. *Factors of Economic Development and the Okovango Delta* 1956. 282 pp. (Research Paper No. 3, Program of Education and Research in Planning, The University of Chicago.)

48. BOXER, BARUCH. *Israeli Shipping and Foreign Trade* 1957. 176 pp.

*49. MAYER, HAROLD M. *The Port of Chicago and the St. Lawrence Seaway*

50. PATTISON, WILLIAM D. *Beginnings of the American Rectangular Land Survey System, 1784–1800* 1957. 2d printing 1963. 260 pp.

*51. BROWN, ROBERT HAROLD. *Political Areal-Functional Organization: With Special Reference to St. Cloud, Minnesota*

52. BEYER, JACQUELYN. *Integration of Grazing and Crop Agriculture: Resources Management Problems in the Uncompahgre Valley Irrigation Project* 1957. 131 pp.

53. ACKERMAN, EDWARD A. *Geography as a Fundamental Research Discipline* 1958. 40 pp. $1.00.

*54. AL-KHASHAB, WAFIQ HUSSAIN. *The Water Budget of the Tigris and Euphrates Basin*

55. LARIMORE, ANN EVANS. *The Alien Town: Patterns of Settlement in Busoga, Uganda* 1958. 210 pp.

56. MURPHY, FRANCIS C. *Regulating Flood-Plain Development* 1958. 216 pp.

*57. WHITE, GILBERT F., *et al. Changes in Urban Occupance of Flood Plains in the United States*

58. COLBY, MARY MC RAE. *The Geographic Structure of Southeastern North Carolina* 1958. 242 pp.

*59. MEGEE, MARY CATHERINE. *Monterrey, Mexico: Internal Patterns and External Relations*

60. WEBER, DICKINSON. *A Comparison of Two Oil City Business Centers (Odessa-Midland, Texas)* 1958. 256 pp.

61. PLATT, ROBERT S. *Field Study in American Geography* 1959. 408 pp.

62. GINSBURG, NORTON, editor. *Essays on Geography and Economic Development* 1960. 196 pp.

63. HARRIS, CHAUNCY D., and FELLMANN, JEROME D. *International List of Geographical Serials* 1960. 247 pp.

64. TAAFFE, ROBERT N. *Rail Transportation and the Economic Development of Soviet Central Asia* 1960. 186 pp.

65. SHEAFFER, JOHN R. *Flood Proofing: An Element in a Flood Damage Reduction Program* 1960. 190 pp.

66. RODGERS, ALLAN L. *The Industrial Geography of the Port of Genova* 1960. 150 pp.

67. KENYON, JAMES B. *Industrial Localization and Metropolitan Growth: The Paterson-Passaic District* 1960. 250 pp.

68. GINSBURG, NORTON. *An Atlas of Economic Development* 1961. 119 pp. 14 × 8½″. Cloth $7.50. University of Chicago Press.

69. CHURCH, MARTHA. *Spatial Organization of Electric Power Territories in Massachusetts* 1960. 200 pp.

70. WHITE, GILBERT F., *et al. Papers on Flood Problems* 1961. 234 pp.

71. GILBERT, E. W. *The University Town in England and West Germany* 1961. 79 pp. 4 plates. 30 maps and diagrams.

72. BOXER, BARUCH. *Ocean Shipping in the Evolution of Hong Kong* 1961. 108 pp.

73. ROBINSON, IRA M. *New Industrial Towns on Canada's Resource Frontier* 1962. (Research Paper No. 4, Program of Education and Research in Planning, The University of Chicago.) 192 pp.

74. TROTTER, JOHN E. *State Park System in Illinois* 1962. 152 pp.

75. BURTON, IAN. *Types of Agricultural Occupance of Flood Plains in the United States* 1962. 167 pp.

76. PRED, ALLAN. *The External Relations of Cities During 'Industrial Revolution'* 1962. 124 pp.

77. BARROWS, HARLAN H. *Lectures on the Historical Geography of the United States as Given in 1933* Edited by WILLIAM A. KOELSCH. 1962. 248 pp.

78. KATES, ROBERT WILLIAM. *Hazard and Choice Perception in Flood Plain Management* 1962. 157 pp.

79. HUDSON, JAMES. *Irrigation Water Use in the Utah Valley, Utah* 1962. 249 pp.

80. ZELINSKY, WILBUR. *A Bibliographic Guide to Population Geography* 1962. 257 pp.

*81. DRAINE, EDWIN H. *Import Traffic of Chicago and Its Hinterland*

*82. KOLARS, JOHN F. *Tradition, Season, and Change in a Turkish Village* NAS-NRC Foreign Field Research Program Report No. 15. 1963. 205 pp.

83. WIKKRAMATILEKE, RUDOLPH. *Southeast Ceylon: Trends and Problems in Agricultural Settlement* 1963. 163 pp.

84. KANSKY, K. J. *Structure of Transportation Networks: Relationships between Network Geometry and Regional Characteristics* 1963. 155 pp.

85. BERRY, BRIAN J. L. *Commercial Structure and Commercial Blight* 1963. 254 pp.

86. BERRY, BRIAN J. L., and TENNANT, ROBERT J. *Chicago Commercial Reference Handbook* 1963. 278 pp.

87. BERRY, BRIAN J. L., and HANKINS, THOMAS D. *A Bibliographic Guide to the Economic Regions of the United States* 1963. 128 pp.

88. MARCUS, MELVIN G. *Climate-Glacier Studies in the Juneau Ice Field Region, Alaska* 1964. 128 pp

89. SMOLE, WILLIAM J. *Owner-Cultivatorship in Middle Chile* 1964. 176 pp.

90. HELVIG, MAGNE. *Chicago's External Truck Movements: Spatial Interaction between the Chicago Area and Its Hinterland* 1964. 132 pp.

*Out of print.

91. HILL, A. DAVID. *The Changing Landscape of a Mexican Municipio, Villa Las Rosas, Chiapas* NAS-NRC Foreign Field Research Program Report No. 26. 1964. 121 pp.

92. SIMMONS, JAMES W. *The Changing Pattern of Retail Location* 1964. 212 pp.

93. WHITE, GILBERT F. *Choice of Adjustment to Floods* 1964. 164 pp.

94. MCMANIS, DOUGLAS R. *The Initial Evaluation and Utilization of the Illinois Prairies, 1815–1840* 1964. 109 pp.

95. PERLE, EUGENE D. *The Demand for Transportation: Regional and Commodity Studies in the United States* 1964. 130 pp.

96. HARRIS, CHAUNCY D. *Annotated World List of Selected Current Geographical Serials in English.* 1964. 32 pp. $1.00

97. BOWDEN, LEONARD W. *Diffusion of the Decision To Irrigate: Simulation of the Spread of a New Resource Management Practice in the Colorado Northern High Plains* 1965. 146 pp.

98. KATES, ROBERT W. *Industrial Flood Losses: Damage Estimation in the Lehigh Valley* 1965. 76 pp.

99. RODER, WOLF. *The Sabi Valley Irrigation Projects* 1965. 213 pp.

100. SEWELL, W. R. DERRICK. *Water Management and Floods in the Fraser River Basin* 1965. (in press)

101. RAY, D. MICHAEL. *Market Potential and Economic Shadow: A Quantitative Analysis of Industrial Location in Southern Ontario* 1965. 164 pp.

102. AHMAD, QAZI. *Indian Cities: Characteristics and Correlates* 1965. 184 pp.